DRAGON
MAGICK

About the Author

A native of the Pacific Northwest, D.J. Conway (1939 - 2019) studied the occult fields for over 35 years. Her quest for knowledge covered every aspect of Paganism and Wicca to New Age and Eastern philosophies; plus history, the magical arts, philosophy, customs, mythologies and folklore. In 1998, she was voted Best Wiccan and New Age author by *Silver Chalice*, a Pagan magazine.

Conway wrote more than 20 nonfiction books, including *Celtic Magic* (Llewellyn), *Dancing with Dragons* (Llewellyn), *Mystical Dragon Magic* (Llewellyn), *The Ancient Art of Faery Magick* (10 Speed Press), and *The Little Book of Candle Magic* (10 Speed Press).

She lived a rather quiet life, with most of her time spent researching and writing.

DRAGON MAGICK

**CALL ON THE CLANS TO
HELP YOUR PRACTICE SOAR**

D.J. CONWAY

x

Llewellyn Publications
Woodbury, Minnesota

FIRST EDITION
Fourth Printing, 2024

Book design by Samantha Penn
Cover design by Shira Atakpu
Cover illustration by John Blumen
Editing by Laura Kurtz
Interior illustrations by Ty Derk

Llewellyn Publications is a registered trademark of Llewellyn Worldwide Ltd.

Library of Congress Cataloging-in-Publication Data
Names: Conway, D. J. (Deanna J.), author. | Llewellyn Publications.
Title: Dragon magick : call on the clans to help your practice soar / D.J. Conway.
Other titles: Dragon magic
Description: First Edition. | Woodbury, Minnesota : Llewellyn Publications, [2019]
Identifiers: LCCN 2019015360 (print) | LCCN 2019980489 (ebook) | ISBN 9780738759531 (alk. paper) | ISBN 9780738760742 (ebook)
Subjects: LCSH: Dragons. | Magic.
Classification: LCC GR830.D7 C659 2019 (print) | LCC GR830.D7 (ebook) | DDC 398.24/54--dc23
LC record available at https://lccn.loc.gov/2019015360
LC ebook record available at https://lccn.loc.gov/2019980489

Llewellyn Worldwide Ltd. does not participate in, endorse, or have any authority or responsibility concerning private business transactions between our authors and the public.

All mail addressed to the author is forwarded, but the publisher cannot, unless specifically instructed by the author, give out an address or phone number.

Any Internet references contained in this work are current at publication time, but the publisher cannot guarantee that a specific location will continue to be maintained. Please refer to the publisher's website for links to authors' websites and other sources.

Llewellyn Publications
A Division of Llewellyn Worldwide Ltd.
2143 Wooddale Drive
Woodbury, MN 55125.2989
www.llewellyn.com

Printed in the United States of America

Other books by D.J. Conway

Magickal, Mystical Creatures
Mystical Dragon Magick
Dancing with Dragons
The Mysterious, Magickal Cat
Guides, Guardians, and Angels

To Cyndi Lou and John for encouragement,
and to all other dragon lovers.

CONTENTS

⊚NE

DRAGONS IN MYTHOLOGY
AND LEGEND

The world's mythologies are full of tales about dragons. Sometimes they are portrayed as huge serpents, sometimes as the type of dragon known to the Western world, sometimes in the shape know to those in East Asia. However, dragons have always played a part in the shaping of this world and its many diverse cultures. They also have had an important role in cultural perception of spiritual ideas.

Dragons have been portrayed in many forms and variations of these forms. Ancient teachings say dragons can have two or four legs or none at all, a pair of wings or be wingless, breathe fire and smoke, and have scales on their bodies. Their blood is extremely poisonous and corrosive but also very magickal. Blood, or the life force, is a symbol of the intensity of their elemental-type energies. Depending upon the reception they received from humans in the area where they lived, dragons could be either beneficial or violent. One thing is for certain: dragons were regarded with awe by all cultures affected by their presence and interaction with humans.

Although one can speak of dragons as a separate species of being, there are numerous subspecies and families within the dragon community, as one can deduce from reading ancient histories and stories. The subspecies and families may have greater or lesser differences in appearance but still retain the basic traits that are common to all dragons wherever they are. One family of dragons with very similar characteristics lived in Europe, specifically in northern Germany, Scandinavia, and islands of the North Atlantic. A second family was recognized in France, Italy, and Spain. A third family dwelt in the British Isles, including Ireland: these dragons, commonly called Firedrakes, included the winged but legless Worm. A fourth family, winged but legless, was found in the Mediterranean area, in Greece, Asia Minor, southern Russia, and northern Africa. A fifth family—the largest in number—was the dragons of China, Pacific Asia, and Indonesia. The sixth family, of very limited size and number, was found in the Americas and Australia.

In the Eastern world, dragons seldom breathe fire and are more benevolent, although hot-tempered and destructive when provoked. They are sometimes pictured as wingless but can propel themselves through the air if they wish. The dragons of Asia, Mexico, the Americas, and Australia propelled themselves through the skies by balancing between the Earth's magnetic field and the winds.

In China, for example, dragons are portrayed with four legs, a long sinuous serpentine body, and a snake-like tail; they range in size from a few feet long up to the Great Chien Tang, who was over a thousand feet in length. They could speak, were able to alter their forms and sizes, and had a varying number of claws.

Chinese emperors adopted the five-clawed dragon as a sacred ancestor and symbol of their power. Only Imperial dragons were said to have the special five claws on each foot. All other Asian dragons had only three or four claws. It became a law that only the Emperor could have a five-clawed dragon embroidered on his robes or painted on anything.

According to tradition, China's history dated back to 3000 BCE, although modern historians only go back to 1600 BCE. A clay vessel from about 2000 BCE is decorated with a dragon picture. The dragon symbol and figure still exist in modern Chinese art and celebrations.

The Chinese divided their dragons into groups or classes, each with different characteristics. There were four major Lung Wang dragons, or Dragon-Kings. The names of these brothers were Ao Kuang, Ao Jun, Ao Shun, and Ao Ch'in. They also had specific duties: the t'ien lung supported the mansion of the gods; the shen lung brought rain; the ti lung controlled the rivers; and the fu-ts'an lung guarded hidden treasures and deposits of precious metals. The Lung Wang, or Dragon Kings, resembled the Indian Nagas, or sacred serpents. They were the patron deities of rivers, lakes, seas, and rain. They had valuable pearls in their throats and lived in magnificent underwater palaces.

Further divisions produced the kiao-lung, or scaled dragon: ying-lung with wings, k'iu-lung with horns, ch'i-lung which was hornless, and the p'an-lung which was earth-bound. The ch'i lung dragon was red, white, and green; the k'iu- lung was green. Chinese dragons were also entirely black, white, red, or yellow, with yellow considered superior.

When it came to using dragons for decoration, there were nine distinct categories: the p'u lao was carved on gongs; the ch'iu niu and pi his on fiddles and literature tablets; the pa hsia at the base of stone monuments; the chao feng on the eaves of temples; the chi'ih on beams of bridges; the suan ni only on the throne of the Buddha; the yai tzu on the hilts of swords; and the pi han on prison gates.

Chinese experts were said to be able to tell the age of Eastern dragons and their origins by their colors. Yellow dragons were believed to be born from yellow gold a thousand years old; blue dragons from blue gold eight hundred years old; and red, white, and black dragons from gold of the same color a thousand years old.

To the Chinese, a dragon could be either male or female. They laid eggs, some of which did not hatch for a thousand years. When a hatching did occur, it was known because of great meteor showers, violent thunderstorms, and great showers of hail.

The number of scales on a dragon was also of importance. Some ancient dragon experts in China maintained that a true dragon has exactly eighty-one scales, while others state that the number was one hundred and seventeen. They were never said to be covered with anything except scales. This is a characteristic of dragons worldwide. However, Western dragons have a varying number of scales and claws. Eastern dragons were also said to be able to fly despite not having wings thanks to the lump on the top of their heads. All dragons have very distinct and individual personalities, just as humans do.

In Chinese medicine, the skin, bones, teeth, and saliva of dragons were considered very valuable. Powdered dragon bone was a magickal cure-all. Old medical textbooks are quick to point out that dragons periodically shed their skin and bones like snakes do. Since the shed skins glowed in the dark, presumably they were easy to locate. Some of the bones were listed as slightly poisonous and could only be prepared in non-iron instruments. The shedding and regrowth of teeth is known to occur among certain mammals, reptiles, and amphibians.

Dragon saliva was said to be found as a frothy foam on the ground or floating on the water. It was usually deposited during mating or fighting. One Chinese story tells of a great battle just off the coast near a fishing village. The villagers watched the great dragons rolling in the black clouds and leaping in the waves for a day and a night. Their echoing roars could be clearly heard. The next morning these people set out in all their fishing boats to the place of the battle. They scooped up whole boatloads of dragon saliva they found floating in huge piles on the ocean's surface.

The blood of Eastern dragons was sometimes red, other times black. Dragon experts said it changed into amber when it soaked into the ground. Wherever dragon blood fell, the ground became incapable of supporting any vegetation. Although the blood was considered dangerous and sometimes deadly in myths of various cultures of Asia, European heroes bathed in it to create invulnerability or drank it to become wise. This transformation of the blood into amber could well be an alchemical expression of the manifestation of magickal power and elemental energies into a desired physical result.

Asian/Eastern dragons did not figure in Chinese creation myths. Only rarely, and then only by accident, did they come in conflict with gods or heroes. These dragons tended to mind their own business and keep a beneficial attitude toward humans. Asian dragons had specific duties, such as controlling the weather and keeping the land and animals fertile, as well as assignments to help humans learn certain civilized arts. Although dragon parts were widely esteemed in traditional Chinese medicine, these magickal creatures were not hunted down as were Western dragons.

In the Mideast, there seems to have been a meeting ground for dragons, some being depicted like Chinese dragons, others more like Western dragons. Both the Greek Medea and Ceres were said to ride in chariots pulled by dragons. Ancient Greece and Rome considered the dragon both beneficent and evil, depending upon the activities of the creature. The purple dragon became the emblem of the Byzantine emperors. These are just a few of the legends and tales of dragons around the world.

All legends agree on certain characteristics concerning dragons, among them that you should never look a dragon in the eyes, as they have hypnotic powers. A dragon is not likely to give you their real name, as doing so would give you power over them—and humans would be incapable of pronouncing it anyway. Several legends from different cultures speak of the draconic ability to appear in human form. When a dragon does shapeshift, it is very difficult to see through his disguise unless he wants you to.

Medieval medicine and magick mention the use of dragon's blood many times. Since real dragon's blood was not available, practitioners had to turn to other sources. Hematite, or "bloodstone" (an ore rich in iron), and the mineral cinnabar (a compound of mercury), were both called forms of dragon's blood. However, the most widely used "dragon's blood" was a gum resin. It was said that these trees originally grew from actual spilled dragon's blood and this legendary heritage even figures into the trees' scientific names: *Dracaena cinnabari* and *Dracaena draco*. Most of these trees are found in the Socotra archipelago of the Arabian sea and the Canary Islands. Their reddish gum resin is still known and used in magickal procedures today.

Dragons are long-lived and very wise, and they hoard treasures and knowledge. The older the dragon, the wiser, but conversing with an old dragon is a double-edged sword: the dragon may be wiser and able to give you greater knowledge, but they are also touchy and extremely untrustworthy unless you handle them correctly. After all, the dragon has been around long enough to have experienced human unreliability and deceit.

Dragons have control of the deeper currents of elemental energies than is usually felt by humans and are always connected in some manner with various forms of the four elements.

Depending upon the behavior of the dragons under observation, their appearance can be considered an omen of good fortune.

Dragons tend to speak in riddles and symbols, avoiding straight answers whenever possible. They do not care for indecisive humans who are afraid to make a decision or take responsibility. Do not make the mistake of trying to physically attack a dragon: the dragon is an astral creature, incapable of being actually harmed by a physical weapon of any kind.

As one can see from the legends, there was a time when dragons materialized from the astral into the physical plane on a fairly regular basis. Considering a dragon's intelligence, it is no wonder they now choose to stay away from humans. Most humans want to control, dissect, or vanquish everything they do not understand ... and even a lot of what they do understand.

However, the wonderful and vast storehouse of dragon magick and power is still available if the magician will take the time to learn how to approach dragons and their deep magickal energies.

SEEKING AND WORKING
WITH DRAGONS

It should be obvious by now that I have a deep respect and love for dragons, a belief in their powers as co-magicians that is backed by years of personal experience. And I hope I have piqued your interest enough to want to work with them.

So how does one go about finding dragons? And how do you use their power? Should you do co-magick with dragons, or should you avoid the partnership?

I assume, since you have read this far, that you either already practice some form of magick or are seriously contemplating doing so. If you are experiencing doubt about your worthiness to work in the area of magick, any area of magick, you have some serious work to do on your self-image and the programming you have undergone that created your poor self-image.

Every magician, indeed every person who even uses prayer, constantly walks the fine line between an overinflated ego and an appreciation of their self-worth. The person understands, without canny cover-ups, exactly why they are choosing to work magick at any given time. This understanding is vital in order to assess the end result of the spellworking, the type of magick used, and the consequences that may be forthcoming for certain actions. What others think of a magician's reasons is not important; they do not pay penalties, gain the advantages of the rituals, or know exactly what the magician may think and feel. However, the magician must know what is deep within her/his own mind and heart and deal with any negative programming or intentions that are selfish and unjustified.

A good magician practices neither white nor black magick exclusively. A good, effective magician is what I call gray, one who understands completely the consequences of actions and is willing to do what is necessary, particularly in the areas of protection and the removal of evil. The effective magician knows themselves like no one else does and must be brutally honest about the real intents and purposes for using any type of magick in the first place, but especially so when practicing dragon magick.

The magician who wishes to practice dragon magick cannot afford any lingering doubts regarding whether they have the right to ask these powerful entities for help. Like many other beings, physical and nonphysical, dragons will take advantage of anyone who wavers in their commitment or who is unclear about their intent of a ritual.

Does this mean that unless you are perfect in all levels of your being that you cannot attract, contact, and learn from dragons? Of course not. But if you desire a continued companionship with them, you must strive to better yourself, balance the ebbs and tides of energies within you, and make this effort an ongoing project. Every magician and spiritual seeker should be aware that there is no such thing as complete perfection within the human body and mind one hundred percent of the time. If you could become that perfect, you would no longer inhabit a physical body. The laws of the universe do not allow anything to remain static, nonmoving, nongrowing. Perfection is static in whatever form it currently has; therefore, in order to confirm to the laws of the universe, that perfect form must evolve into something else, some form of being that can continue to evolve to the next higher stage of life. Change is one of the few constants of universal law.

So how does one go about finding dragons? You begin by learning as much about dragons and their magickal habits as possible. Then look at your reasons for wishing to practice dragon magick with an objective and critical eye. When you feel comfortable with these steps—and only then—you begin building an atmosphere that will attract dragons. You perform certain actions that arouse their curiosity and draw them to your vicinity. You beam a mental welcome, setting aside time and place to communicate with them on the astral level through mental visualization and speech. You also must believe they exist, even if you cannot see them with your physical eyes or prove their existence to someone else.

If you wish to attract dragons, you have to cast aside social taboos you may have regarding "seeing things" and know with your heart that dragons *do* exist. Mentally invite the dragons to make their presence known by thought or deed. Be sensitive and extra aware of what is occurring around you. Most dragons tend to be subtle in their first contacts with humans. They may choose to make an appearance in dreams, or as flashes of movement seen in peripheral vision. They can even be as subtle as a hovering presence behind you, looking over your shoulder.

Guardian dragons, the easiest to contact, often appear as little voices or faces and forms in the mind. Dragons may show up unannounced at any time, but especially during meditation or magickal rituals, either singly or several at a time. They love the power flow of ritual and will make an appearance just to bathe in the energy. They may well have been there all the time but you simply did not notice them…not surprising, since dragons are masters at concealment.

The smaller dragons delight in sharing the vibrations of tarot, rune, and other readings. One of my guardian dragons likes to play with my crystal pendulum. He either bats at it with a claw or mentally sends it spinning in nonsense directions. The only solution to using the pendulum is to let him tire of his game before attempting to get a reliable answer. He and his companions like to peer over my shoulder during tarot readings, muttering their own interpretations all the while. One just has to be patient with them, as you would with a small and curious child.

You have to be willing to practice a great deal of patience, self-control, and self-discipline, learning to work within a specific set of magickal laws in order to consistently attract and elicit the help of dragons. As with all magickal procedures, nothing is cast in stone, but there are certain aspects of these procedures that cannot be eliminated or changed to any great extent without disturbing the flow of magickal power.

Casting aside the magickal laws for working with dragon power is certain to get you into trouble. Even the most positive dragon is a wily beast who, like many humans, tends to look out for themselves first. Dragons likely developed this attitude after trying to work with humans thousands of years ago and finding puny mortals to be unreliable and often treacherous allies.

Your attitude toward the existence of dragons must be the first big step in preparation for meeting them. The power of dragons is a tremendous force that can amplify a magician's ability to new heights.

Why bother cultivating the cooperation and companionship of dragons? Because their wisdom and elemental-type energies are unequaled, boundless. By means of their extremely long lives and unique thought-processes, they have access to forgotten information and knowledge, especially in the field of magick. Dragon power also helps the magician to make personal, inner changes that may be necessary. Helping to remove past negative programming or any self-destructive habits is well within the abilities of dragons; of course, the human involved must desire those changes. Like all magick, dragon magick does not produce miraculous results without work.

Dragons can create opportunities, provide encouragement and guidance, and even back the magician into a figurative corner so that they must face problems and make decisions. But they will never do for you what you should do for yourself. Once befriended, dragons make excellent protectors and powerful fellow magicians.

A true knowledge-seeking magician weighs all possibilities for use in their magick, keeping what feels right and discarding the rest. Likewise, dragon magick is not for all. Dragon magick is only for the self-disciplined seeker who realizes the potential dangers and yet dares to communicate with and befriend this vast astral power of the ages. It is for the magician who is serious about changing their life and the living space around them. It is an asset for those who can give love and trust (not blindly but with common sense), and have a desire for true friendship.

If you use dragon magick for unjustified purposes or try to manipulate and control dragons, you can expect a terrific negative backlash. In the matters of self-protection or bringing justice down upon dangerous members of society, I have absolutely no second thoughts about employing dragons. As to manipulation and control, one simply does not do that with friends and co-magicians. Common sense tells you that such behavior will terminate the friendship and cause other magicians to cease their cooperation or perhaps even work against you. If you prove yourself to be a danger to dragons, they are likely to ensorcel you such that your magick does not work.

What if you have attracted a dragon or dragons who make you feel uncomfortable? I have known this to occur with other spiritual guides, so I suppose it can also happen with dragons, although I have not personally experienced this. If a dragon makes you uncomfortable, it is very likely that you are not ready yet to work with its energies. First, become clear in your own mind why you feel this discomfort. Perhaps the actual root of the discomfort is a bit of programming struggling to make itself felt and keep control over your activities. Perhaps the dragon's coloring has triggered old conditionings. A black dragon produces this feeling in people who have been taught that dragons—particularly black dragons—are evil. The farther into the subconscious you dig, the more you'll be amazed at what is in there, controlling your thoughts and actions when you least expect it.

If you still feel uncomfortable, set aside a time for a brief meditation and mental conversation with the dragon. Explain carefully and politely that you are attempting to remedy the situation, but at this time you just do not feel that the two of you can work positively together. Project as much good will as you can. The dragon will understand.

Like the old mapmakers who wrote "Here be dragons" on the unknown edges of their maps, I wish you a safe journey into dragon country. Go, and be prepared for a fantastic voyage on which you can make new friends and magick-working partners. You will be pleasantly surprised at the knowledge you will learn. Go prepared to wrest what you want from the astral plane, and you may very likely have an unprofitable journey filled with unpleasant experiences. Would-be conquering invaders have never been met with friendship, no matter their plane of existence. Exploring traders who were willing to listen and bargain a bit always had the most successful profitable voyage of discovery. Travel into dragon country with caution, an open mind, and friendship in your heart. The journey will be well worth it.

ᵀHREE

DRAGON POWER
IN MAGICK

Working with dragons in magick is different in many ways from other magickal procedures, but not so different that you can disregard certain rules. You need to know how to practice visualization, meditation, and self-discipline; have a good sense of ethics and absolute truthfulness with yourself; and maintain a sense of consistency in practice. All of these values and skills are important components of any magickal system, but they are a must when working with dragons. Remember that there must be an exchange of energies in your workings together.

Visualization begins with unlearning many of the so-called value systems heaped on us by other people, the most common of which is that use of the imagination and day-dreaming are unproductive and bad. True, overuse of the imagination and frequent daydreaming are negative if they occupy most of your life and time; if you daydream about what you want to happen instead of planning and taking action, then you are avoiding responsibility. However, for any type of magick to become truly effective, you must learn how to vividly picture in your mind the event or result that you wish for. Once you firmly have the outcome in your mind, you perform your rituals and then release the mental energy for manifestation.

Self-discipline and ethics go together. A magician should not, for their own good, dabble in controlling other people or indulge in questionable personal behavior. Jealousy, envy, lust, greed, and anger should not control what a magician does during ritual. In fact, these undesirable emotions should not control any part of a magician's life. These intense emotions tend to cloud judgment and either bring emotional backlash on the magician or cause deliberate harm to others, which in itself brings eventual backlash or retribution upon the magician—it is not worth the misery, either way.

A magician must sincerely desire whatever they are asking for in rituals. If the wish is half-hearted with little emotional intensity behind it, the dragons (or any other entities for that matter) will simply not be interested in helping. And do not think you can pull one over on spiritual or astral plane entities—they can see *right* to the truth ... and the truth is never hidden from dragons.

One of the worst things a magician can do is to take something away from another person by means of magick: this includes health, property, life, or freedom. Loss of freedom is acceptable only for criminals. Very often I find that beginning magicians want to control another's decisions and life on the subject of love. Forget it! The price for doing this kind of manipulative magick is too high. If the person was meant to love you, they would already show interest. Any magician considering such a use of magick had better take a long, truthful look at their true motives.

The second part of the use of magick is that the magician must release the emotions and desire after the ritual is finished. To constantly think about what you want accomplished binds the energies to you such that they cannot manifest. To constantly talk about your desires or to talk about the rituals you are performing to get them will surely keep them from manifestation. To want something so much you can taste it and yet not care if you get it is a very difficult mood to cultivate. Getting as close to this attitude as possible is what is important.

There must be an exchange of energies between the physical, emotional, mental, and spiritual planes for any spellwork to result in a manifestation. Playing at ritual magick, particularly dragon magick, will not get you anywhere. Without mental concentration, physical working, emotional involvement, and intensity of purpose, in other words, dragons will not be interested in adding their vast energies to yours. Dragons are attracted by the energies you raise during ritual, a kind of astral pay-off since they "feed" on this energy.

Belief in powers beyond yourself is important in any kind of magick. There is an old saying: "Whether you believe you can or you believe you can't, you are right." We may not understand

how these powers and energies work; we may not be able to de-
scribe them to anyone. But we magicians know they exist. A magician believes in them because they see the results of their use.

Every magician who wishes to be effective in ritual and
manifestation, who desires to grow and expand in knowledge,
sooner or later comes to the conclusion that magick is a very
serious practice. They learn to set aside time for study and
self-improvement through meditation. They practice what are
commonly called the psychic arts: tarot, runes, the pendulum,
crystal reading, dream analysis, and so on. They cultivate the
senses, especially observation, which includes what is in both
the physical and astral realms. They learn to read their own intuitive feelings and the vibrations of others.

Not all dragons are the same, no more than humans are.
They each have their own specific individuality and personality.
Different dragon clans have different interests. There are very
general descriptions of dragon interests and abilities, as draconic abilities overlap in many areas. It is best to work with a
balance of types of dragons, with one particular dragon aspect
predominating according to the intent of the ritual. Above all,
a magician must know themselves—all habits good and bad—
and face them squarely. There cannot be any self-delusion if ritual is to be effective and positive in nature.

The next logical step in the process for being balanced is
to seek spiritual enlightenment. After all, when the very foun-
dation of magick and ritual is finally uncovered, the magician
finds that all ritual and spellwork is meant to be a means for
spiritual growth and development. We are each responsible

for the choices we make in life, even down to being here in the first place. We have no right to place any blame on others for what is going wrong in our lives. If you make a wrong decision, change it and learn from the experience. Working with dragons can make this life path a little easier and a lot more interesting.

FOUR

DRAGON LIVES: FACTS AND FALLACIES

When I finished my second dragon book, I could not imagine there being anything further to learn or say about dragons. How wrong I was! I had only exposed the tip of the iceberg. The more humans on this plane who opened themselves to the reality of dragons, the more dragons of other timelines and levels became aware of us. It turned out to be a fortuitous situation, especially for the endangered dragons of other multiversal levels. They were facing both a pandemic and a physical genocide by other creatures. By May 2010, at least eighteen new clans had escaped to Earth, and since then there have been others. Now, suddenly, we needed to study all the old and new dragon clans, so we can all coexist in peace and harmony.

Many people are fascinated by dragons. The wonderful thing is, everyone who believes in dragons can attract and make friends with these beautiful, powerful, intelligent creatures. Everyone can attract a guardian dragon, one of the smaller, younger members of the species. Guardians, the tiny hatchlings, and the slightly older younglings will usually be the first dragons you meet and work with. Learning to relate to humans and working with human magicians is part of these young dragons' training. Apprenticeship in any trade or study must begin somewhere, so how appropriate to match beginning magicians with guardian dragons under the tutelage of older co-magicians.

The first dragon clans returned to Earth with the humanoids who settled Atlantis and raised the civilization level of the humans here, as I wrote in *Mystical Dragon Magick* (2012). Those clans decided to stay after the fall of Atlantis but eventually had to withdraw to Dragon World in the Otherworld when humans turned violently against them.

Dragons think of time in terms of hundreds and thousands of years, while our idea of time-concept runs to the hundreds. This is because dragons live so much longer than the normal human does. Puberty for dragons starts at about one hundred seventy-five to two hundred years. How and what they are taught, I've yet to get a clear answer. Likely they are taught their clan's history along with specific knowledge about whatever area they desire and in which they have an ability.

Physiology

Dragons are not reptiles, although they appear that way to humans. Their true origins lie elsewhere on other planets in distant galaxies. They are mammalian even though they lay eggs, have scales, and don't suckle their young. We have our own earthly similarity in the duckbilled platypus and the echidna. Their jaws are disarticulated, similar to snakes. There are also other differences, according to clan, in their eyes, spikes, and other body parts.

It is questionable if wyverns (dragonlike creatures whose front two "legs" are their wings) are or have ever been part of dragon clans. At this point, I've yet to see any wyverns among the clans. There are no multi-headed dragons; those are called hydras, a very different magickal creature. Some think the legendary Tiamat is multi-headed but legends don't say she is. She moves her head so fast at times she almost looks as if she has more than one head.

Dragons have a nictitating membrane at the inner angle or beneath the lower eyelid that is capable of extending across the entire eye. Their vision is superb, and they do not suffer from colorblindness. They also have human-like, opposable thumb-claws, even if they have three or up to seven other claw-fingers. Dragons can be right- or left-handed, just like humans. The few dragons with two sets of eyes developed these to avoid being prey on their original planet of existence. As dragons are hunters, all dragon eyes are set in the front of the skull to see forward.

Dragons shed claw sheaths, scales, teeth, and even bones on occasion. Like cats, dragons shed claw coverings. It is also possible for their scales, spikes, and teeth to break and thus be shed for regrowth. If a dragon breaks a bone, it sheds pieces of the old bone as it regrows a new one. Rarely do they leave pieces of birth shells, as most female dragons eat the eggshells after babies have hatched.

Female dragons can hold any position that a male does. There is no definite consistent way to distinguish a female from a male dragon. In other words, coloring, size, and manner of speaking do not help you distinguish. Some dragons banded together as a clan because they are so few. However, that doesn't mean they mate beyond their related species. Like many of the Scottish clans in human history, the banding of several agreeable clans gives them great bargaining power in the High Council, a group that will be discussed later.

Courtship, Breeding, and Young

In a variety of shapes, sizes, and temperaments, dragons were known in ancient cultures and folktales around the world. These dragons are always depicted as fully grown, although dragon nests with eggs are sometimes mentioned. Eggs certainly mean baby dragons, yet the tales rarely mention them. Logically, there must be baby dragons (hatchlings, younglings, and fledglings) growing up somewhere, just as there are beginning dragon magicians trying their best to become more proficient. The smaller guardian (or fledgling) dragons can range from calf- to waist-high. They can become a type of astral watchdog for you, your family, pets, and property.

Breeding dragon females consume great amounts of seashells (calcium), granite, and marble before, during, and after laying eggs. Although dragons may seem to sample human-type food, they only take certain essences of the food. Amazingly enough, dragons appear to love the essence of chocolate, the darker the better. Others have noted the same propensity between fairies and chocolate. Relatedly, the psychological effects of oils and incense are very great, particularly among the different dragon clans. However, do not use poppy! Dragons are allergic to poppy.

Unlike with lizards, the sex of hatchlings is not dependent on the degree of heat at the hatching place. Dragons are male or female determined by their DNA, just as humans are. However, dragons cannot sexually mix with humans; there are no human-dragon hybrids. Humans cannot become dragons for any reason, nor would the dragons want it that way. They are an extremely intelligent species, able to access significantly more information about all things than humans can. They have powers in some categories that humans can only dream about at this stage of our evolution. The most humans can do at this point is to acknowledge their existence, work with them on magickal and spiritual projects, gain their trust, and develop life-long friendships.

All dragons mate while flying in the corridor space between this realm and the astral realm. That space is like a split between space and reality. As far as I can determine, this corridor space does not exist all the time but is created by the dragons as they need it. This space is also used as gateways to other time-lines and galaxy levels.

At the very edges of this split is what is called shadow energy. It exists at the thin edge between dark and light energies and is only used with the help of certain dragon clans. It is a difficult energy to use properly but can mask spells with illusion so that they cannot be interfered with by others. It is not dark or evil energy and will not mask dark spells. This is the energy used by a dedicated Shadow Walker or War Walker, a title applied to humans who hunt down and remedy or destroy evil.

Dragons court their mates. If either one decides to end it during the courting time, there is usually a calm separation. A few dragons never mate for life. Once two dragons decide to become a pair, it is for life, unless one is killed or dies. The remaining one can seek another mate. However, no dragon will get involved with another's mate. That would be a breach of clan honor, which would then require the involvement of the High Council. Honor is very important to dragons, although the definition of honor may vary slightly from clan to clan.

Courtship is discouraged before training is finished, which is usually about age four hundred to five hundred years. Each clan council keeps meticulous mating records to avoid inbreeding. There are only a few special cases on matings between different clans; these kinds of mating are carefully considered by the High Council before permission is granted. The physical matings all take place in that thin sliver of space between this world and the Otherworld, as far as I can determine from communicating with some of the females. Eggs take two to three years to grow before they are laid. Then it takes another human year to hatch. It is unusual for a dragon to have more than two eggs in a clutch. Dragons seem to practice their own form of birth control, or their fertility rate is governed by their DNA.

Most dragon hatchlings start out life being a much lighter shade of scale color than the parents. They darken as they age. For example, a young dragon who is fire-engine red with tan on the wing membranes will end up a red so dark as to appear almost black, with membranes a deep, rich, earth brown marked with spots of black, like camouflage gear. In size, regular hatchlings are usually small, some as small as six inches long. Two clans have much tinier hatchlings because the adults are not very large at all. These clans are the Tam-Jin-Kee and the Galaxy Rainbows. Hatchlings are the equivalent of human ages from birth to seven, although their antics can be hilarious. They are typical of that age range in humor, rough play, short attention span, and the tendency to ask questions and crave attention. You will need a lot of patience, a solid sense of humor, and large amounts of understanding when in the company of hatchlings.

Generally speaking, if you find yourself in the company of hatchlings and younglings, consider yourself privileged. The little younglings, although always accompanied by an adult somewhere nearby, are placed with responsible humans to learn how to interact with us. This is part of their training, until they are old enough to become guardians or take on other duties.

Small dragons are actually excellent catchers of small demons, negative creatures, and balls of negative energy. Little dragons eating negative energy is rather like a human child eating candy. The only difference appears to be that the dragons don't get indigestion from overeating.

The smaller dragons belch little fireballs when they hiccup, belch, or burp, and have a propensity to snack on socks and shoes when cutting teeth. They have been known to leave soft scales on toothbrushes and hair brushes when they use them to scratch their itchy shedding skin. They also "borrow" shiny objects, such as jewelry, desk pens, car keys, and fishing lures, because they haven't yet learned not to do this. The borrowing can become extensive, especially if the objects are shiny or un-usual. Quartz crystals are very fascinating to them.

Certain dragons, both males and females, are voice-tested for singing and chanting, both positive and negative spells. These include dragons of all clans. They may be petitioned for help through clan leaders, who then take it to the Great Council. The entire clans then discuss the request and make the de-cision—yes or no. It is rare that this dragon skill is ever used at human requests. The only times I've heard their music, but never seen, have been at the solstices and equinoxes. I assume it is part of their special celebrations in some fashion.

Dragons and Humans

All dragons hide their true names from humans. Names have tremendous power that can be used against them. Humans can't pronounce complicated dragon or clan names anyway, so we are told names that closely resemble clan or individual personalities and powers. True names are a combination of musical notes and ordinary dragon speech. This is why certain dragons or clans can become curious of certain humans who might chance upon a few musical combinations, either of voice or through an instrument.

Since dragons age differently than humans, they remain in certain stages of growth for much longer periods of time. As mentioned, dragons think of aging in terms of hundreds and thousands of years, as they live far longer than humans do.

So many things are invisible to human eyes. So many things are not what you think they are. Like with many subjects, the more you learn about dragons, the more interesting they become. However, people have some erroneous ideas about them. The adult Western dragons were always on guard against aggressive knights and villagers who wanted the thrill and notoriety of killing a dragon. No wonder Western European, Mexican, and Central American dragons considered humans dangerous. These dragons tended to attack first, thus eliminating surprise raids on their lairs. However, dragon clans differ as to availability and aloofness, and there are clan personalities as well as individual personalities. The Far Eastern dragons are a distinctly different and more benevolent type, working well with the people of China, Indonesia, Japan, and similar cultures. These dragons are honored today by the dragon dance winding through the streets during the celebration of the Chinese New Year.

"Appearing" doesn't mean actually having a dragon manifest physically in front of you, although that can happen. Appearing is more like sensing a presence close to or behind you. Ordinarily, beginners will see them with their inner eyes or as a fleeting movement in the corner of the eye, or in pictures in the mind. Dragon conversations are most often by telepathy.

You will know the thoughts are not yours, because the words, tones, and information are not in your style of thinking.

Dragons have auras just as humans do, which is why one can feel their presence. When two human auras touch, your subconscious mind knows it. So it makes sense that dragons and humans would feel the same effect. That said, dragons do not think like humans or make their choices according to human ethics. Many of them will not even work magick with humans or spend time with us. There is no way any human has enough power or knowledge to enslave a dragon or force one to do your bidding.

Never tell or order a dragon to do anything. Don't call yourself a dragon rider or say that you hold a special position among dragons. Dragons will give you your position, name, or title if and when they think you have earned it. They act as co-magicians or teachers and are not at your beck and call. Likewise, you *never* train dragons to do anything. If you overstep the boundaries of their rules, they leave you stumbling in false delusions until you finally catch on. Then you go back to the training place where you went astray and start learning over again.

Will you see these dragons with your physical eyes? Very rarely. You are more likely to sense their presence. After you acknowledge their presence by noting these actions, the hatchlings, younglings, and guardians will begin to appear in mental pictures. After all, dragons have their actual being in the Otherworld, a realm of much high vibrations than our earthly plane. They temporarily lower these higher vibrations to work with humans.

Sometimes dragons refuse to teach or work with you because you have more to learn and might not be respectful enough. They might work with you later. This is quite common with the new clans who had to come through the Veil from other levels. They have had little or no contact with humanoids.

Different clans and groups within a clan use different marks for magick and communication. Sometimes these symbols briefly appear on their scales. Some dragons appear to appreciate the light sounds of a tambourine, drum, harp, and other instruments. This may be because their own language sounds like a combination of musical notes and a guttural speech. Since we humans don't understand them, especially when learning dragon magick, they display magickal symbols on their scales. This is rather like flash cards for human children.

The proper etiquette with dragons is to treat them with respect but not in a "worshipful" way. Treat them as you would any special tutor or teacher. Prepare yourself mentally and spiritually for dragon magick. And do be cautious when working with certain clans. Some enjoy tricking you with riddles. Others can be very abrupt and impatient, while still others don't wish to be bothered by humans and are short-tempered.

Although healers are found in the great clans, there are certain clans that seem to have specialized in healing for millennia. Teachers from the healing clans often seem to befriend humans who are also healers or may be potential healers.

The ethics of using dragon magick are very strict about bullying with dragons, fire fights, or threats of such. No dragon will participate, and probably all that will happen is that the dragons will cease all work with you. Humans who insist on trying to use dragons for such tactics soon have no real teachers and are avoided as unteachable.

Dragons do not tolerate saddles or harnesses of any kind. If they choose a bonded rider, dragons have the ability to turn certain scales to support the knees, feet, and hands. However, bonded riders are incredibly rare.

All disputes, trials, and major decisions are made by the council. The council is ordinarily comprised of the Elders, but these can be replaced by clan vote for certain reasons. There is a council for each clan to judge breaking of the rules of that clan. If problems are experienced between clans, the dispute is then taken before the higher council, which is made up of an elder from each clan.

Humans cannot physically or astrally become dragons, be born as "hidden dragons," or become masters of dragons. On very rare occasions, a few humans (for reasons only known to the dragons) are temporarily given an ability to assume dragon form on the astral plane only. This is probably done to give us a taste of what it is like to glide, see, and feel things like a dragon does. The dragon can take away this trait as quickly as they gave it, if you misuse it. Likewise, dragons do not become humans. Humans are far below their intelligence, and our memory of history and the past is much shorter. We are thus slower to foresee the possibilities of action and reaction to things we do or want to do.

Dragons are very cunning creatures who have had a turbulent history in the far past with humans. They also have a myriad of personalities, even among clans, just as humans do. Some are not all that friendly with humans, while others become interested only after much observation and careful communication. Some of the last darker clans are very suspicious and only trustworthy after much minor interaction. Humans who are arrogant or pushy or treat dragons disrespectfully as a species to be ordered about are discarded as not worthy of working with or teaching. Honor is very important to dragons, although definitions of honor may be slightly different according to clan.

A guardian dragon, as discussed, is an adolescent or fledgling who is learning to work with humans. Although they lack the size, strength, and knowledge of the older, larger dragons, guardians help humans (particularly magicians) by protecting, aiding in spells and rituals, and in the development of meditation and psychic arts, especially divination. The hatchlings and younglings that reside with you may not be from the same dragon clan. This also is part of their training. A few will be siblings from the same hatchling, but most will not be. It is customary to get acquainted with a guardian dragon before you meet the larger dragons. However, that order may change if the older dragons wish it.

Personal guardian dragons come in various colors, shapes, and sizes, and are of the fledgling age. Often they are in lighter shades and with a myriad of hues on the belly scales. They more or less serve an apprenticeship as part of their learning about humans and their own magick, thus strengthening their own powers. Their scales are softer than those of the adults.

and sometimes barely discernable. To encourage them to join in your rituals, chant just before you begin:

> *Little dragons, rainbow bright,*
> *Good friends of this family,*
> *Send good wishes to us all.*
> *Join our rituals merrily.*
> *Protect us through each day and night,*
> *While awake or while asleep.*
> *Through your love and vigilance,*
> *Do this family safely keep.*

There are often much smaller, younger dragons with the guardian. These are usually very young hatchlings who need a dragon-sitter. The babies are most often about the length of your hand. Colors vary in all the younger dragons, revealing that the babies and guardians often come from different clans. These smaller dragons are lighter in color and their scales soft to the touch, again a small clue to their young age. Older dragons usually have defined scales and sharper, darker coloring.

Dragons do respond in power to moon phases, equinoxes, solstices, and eclipses of both moon and sun. I assume their original planets had the equivalent of these time periods, and therefore their responses have remained to match our equivalent.

GUARDIAN DRAGON MEDITATION

Sit in a comfortable chair with your feet flat on the floor and your hands in your lap. Make certain you will not be disturbed by pets, children, or other people. You may decide to play soft instrumental music to mask background noises.

Take three slow, deep breaths, relaxing more of your body's muscles each time. Visualize yourself surrounded by white light. Your body relaxes more and more until you feel light and very comfortable. See yourself standing beside a well. If anything or anyone in your life is upsetting you, drop it or them into the well. They fall down into the darkness away from you. Walk away, leaving the problems behind you.

You find yourself walking out onto a green lawn in warm sunshine. Under a tree nearby is a garden bench. You decide to sit there and look at the countryside around you. Small dragons of various sizes are playing in the flowers and trees. They begin to watch you, curious about your appearance in their realm.

Soon, several fledglings approach you cautiously, sending you telepathic messages as to your purpose. You easily use telepathy to tell them you are looking for a guardian dragon with which to work. A much larger adult dragon is now observing you from afar, making certain the little ones are safe.

The guardian dragons ask what you want to learn and plan to do. You talk together for a time, enjoying the sunshine and the company. Gradually, the little dragons drift off to play and wrestle in the soft grass. Only one stays behind to talk to you and asks you if you accept their offer to be your guardian dragon. When you answer "yes," the little guardian sends you happy thoughts before running to the adult to finalize the bonding. The little dragon returns to tell you that they will join you very soon, in your next meditation. Bubbling with excitement, the guardian gives you their name and tells you they are anxious to be with you. The little one then runs off to share this news with the other little dragons.

You stand up to leave and find yourself slipping easily into your physical body. You slowly stretch your arms and legs. Your meditation is ended.

◎   ◎   ◎

There will be a time of getting acquainted with your guardian dragon before an adult appears to offer to be a co-magician. The guardian, however, can help with small spells such as protection of you, your family, and pets; getting a parking space; and other less powerful spells. This is an excellent time to get your friendship off to a good start and to observe how small dragons behave.

As for appearance, guardian dragons are usually about knee-high and have had some previous training and preparation. Temperament-wise, they need far less supervision from their elders. Not every young dragon passes the test to take on this responsibility.

Guardian dragons can help in your studies; they also like cloud-busting for fun, sending messages, attracting friends, mind-viewing (what the dragons call meditation), or finding lost objects (which they may have borrowed in the first place). As the two of you grow in friendship and the skills of working with each other, the guardian can aid with more difficult things, such as gaining self-confidence, improving your health, changing your luck into a more positive path, finding the perfect job or career, protecting your family and property, and even discovering true love and friendships.

FIVE

BONDING AND COMMUNICATING

Oone of the first things you need to do is bond with your guardian dragon. You bond with them by mentally acknowledging their existence and asking for their help. Friendship and bonding make it much easier to attract a co-magician dragon, as well as introduce yourself to all the other dragons. Don't expect warm welcomes from the other dragons until they get to know you, and some not even then. Like humans, dragons each have individual personalities, along with their personal likes and dislikes. Many have had no previous contact with humans or humanoids; if they are familiar with humanoids, their experiences may not have been the best, so they avoid humans. When you acknowledge the presence of your guardian dragon, you can actively practice magick together, build a strong friendship, or both. Should both happen, you are to be congratulated on your patience and perseverance.

Dragons prefer to use telepathy when communicating with you. They may begin by sending you mental pictures of symbols and sigils, since this is the easiest method. Sigils (pronounced sĭ-jils) are a type of symbol that represents more than an alphabet or object. The word comes from the Latin *sigillum*, which translates to mean seal or signature. The seal of an Otherworld being or of a spirit is not only its signature, but its phone number and address rolled into one. In some cases, the sigil is synonymous with the Otherworld being itself.

Symbols speak directly to the subconscious mind, which helps because the conscious and subconscious mind (or right and left sides of the brain) have difficulty communicating. Symbols appeal to all the senses at the same time, helping the message get through.

If you prefer to experience and not have to remember the order of things in meditations given in this book, record them first so you can play while meditating. Then you can open yourself to everything you see, hear, and experience without worry. Meditation is simple, once you grasp the relaxing part. Practice and regular meditation soon solve the relaxation problem. You will become so engrossed with what happens in the Otherworld that you won't have time to worry. Don't concern yourself that what you see might be an illusion, because it isn't. All your inner senses, which duplicate the senses you use every day, will come alive in the Otherworld. All of it is truly happening, simply on another level of vibration.

DRAGON MEDITATION

In preparation for meditation, choose a time and place where you will not be disturbed.

You will not be aware of time, because time is a concept that humans have invented. You are also unlikely to be fully aware of what is happening around you, unless the mind senses dangers. In this case, you will be able to return to your body at once. The same applies if you are fearful of anything you see during this time. You are never trapped, caught, in danger of losing your soul, or whatever else people fear; you can open your eyes any time and be back in normal time and place.

Sit in your chair with your feet flat on the floor with your hands in your lap. Take slow, deep breaths, relaxing more of your body's muscles each time. Visualize yourself surrounded by brilliant white light with your guardian spirits at your side. Your body relaxes more and more until you feel light and very comfortable. Feel yourself standing beside a well. If anything or anyone in life is upsetting you, drop it or them into the well. They fall down into the darkness away from you. Walk away from the well, leaving every annoying person and event behind.

You walk across a velvety green lawn toward a huge wooden gate in a wall. The gate is bound with iron scrollwork and hinges, the sunlight bright upon it. As you stand looking at the massive door, you reach up to pull the heavy chain attached to a bell. A deep sound echoes over and over until the door slowly opens. You walk through and become aware of a world before you that has an infinite variety of terrains and lights and shadow. In the far distance is a long range of high mountains; some have snow, a couple are belching volcanic clouds. To one side is a rolling plain with trees and a small river. To the other side are beaches and a calm-looking ocean. You see movement on the ground and in the water and air…large gliding figures. You realize these figures are actually dragons.

Give yourself as much time as you need to explore this strange new world. As soon as you think of a place, you will be transported there. Be polite if you should approach a dragon. Whenever you are finished for this time, think of the gate and find yourself instantly returing there. The gate opens and you step through. Instantly, you find yourself back inside your physical body. Move your fingers and feet slowly until you feel comfortable once more on the physical plane. The mediation is ended.

As time has no meaning to dragons, they have a firm grasp of planetary energy on every level of the Multiverse and the spiritual vibrations behind it all. However, they do seem to acknowledge the planet Earth's equinoxes, solstices, new and full moons, and eclipses, as similar ones do appear in one form or another on every planet in the Multiverse. And each season has a dragon responsible for its energies.

Your co-magician dragon is the best guide you will have to meet other dragons, such as those of the seasons, the elements, and planets, which are important to your spellwork.

The dragons are aware of the energy flows changing when the Earth moves from one season into another. These times are especially powerful since so many spiritual paths have celebrated them for thousands of years.

Spring Equinox: The dragon Eiglis is a yellowish spring green. She works with the air element and the dragon Sairys. This time of year is good for doing work related to the mental realm. This season is useful for beginning new ideas or cycles that will require longer periods of time to complete, so this time is ideal for self-improvement efforts, creating motivation, changes in career or housing, improving material status, setting future goals, and strengthening yourself spiritually.

Summer Solstice: The dragon Suuriy glows a garnet red and works with the fire element and the dragon Fafnir. He is best for anything involving the realm of action. At this time of year, the energy flows are longer and faster now. This is a good season to store vibrational energy by knots in a red cord for use when Earth's tides become low. Continue to work on long-term spells and goals.

Autumn Equinox: The dragon Shadalyn appears a smoky brown color and works with the water element and the dragon Naelyon. She is most useful for matters related to the emotional realm. As the tides of Earth energy begin to slow, it is yet possible to store energy by means of knots in a blue cord.

Winter Solstice: The dragon Aettall is a very watery blue. He works with the earth element and the dragon Grael. Around winter is good for things related to the physical realm. This is the ideal time for practicing divination and physically and spiritually cleaning your house and life; set goals for the next year. Do short-term spells that will be ready to manifest close to the next Spring Equinox.

To attune yourself to the seasons, seriously consider how you relate to each season, which will require deep truthfulness. If your guardian dragon has some mental input, consider it carefully. Perhaps you tried to manifest something in the wrong season or didn't consider the moon phases and planetary days/hours. We humans get our minds set on something we want manifested and often don't consider taking advantage of all the parts that should go into a spell.

Your guardian can be a big help in this and any spellwork. And the more you interact with your guardian dragon, the stronger the bond between you becomes. Working together also prepares you for the more intense co-magician work that will eventually come into your life.

CO-MAGICIAN MEDITATION

In preparation for meditation, choose a time and place where you will not be disturbed.

You will not be aware of time. Nor are you likely to be fully aware of what is happening around you, unless the mind senses dangers. In this case, you will be able to return to your body at once. The same applies if you are fearful of anything you see during this time. You are never trapped, caught, in danger of losing your soul, or whatever else people fear; you can open your eyes any time and be back in normal time and place.

Sit in your chair with your feet flat on the floor with your hands in your lap. Take slow, deep breaths, relaxing more of your body's muscles each time. Visualize yourself surrounded by brilliant white light, with your guardian spirits at your side. Your body relaxes more and more until you feel light and very comfortable. Feel yourself standing beside a well. If anything or anyone in life is upsetting you, drop it or them into the well. They fall down into the darkness away from you. Walk away from the well, leaving every annoying person and event behind.

You find yourself once more at the huge iron-bound gates that lead into the dragon world. With your guardian dragon at your side as a companion and guide, you ring the bell that hangs to one side of the doors.

A fully grown dragon opens the gates and tells you to enter. You tell him that you are looking for a co-magician. "You will find those willing to be co-magicians near the waterfall," he tells you.

As he closes the gates, your guardian dragon looks up at you, then leads the way down a path lined with flowers and tall trees. You hear the splash and trickle of water ahead. As you and your guardian round a corner in the path, you see ahead a gently falling stream of water over moss-covered rocks. Around the pool below the waterfall are many full-grown dragons sitting in the sun or sleeping nearby. The buzz of telepathy you heard at first falls silent as the huge dragons turn to look at you.

"My friend has come to ask if one of you will be a co-magician," your little guardian says.

"Yes, please," you say. "I need help to learn dragon magick."

You feel the dragons gently reading through your thoughts and assessing your desires and potential. Finally, one dragon moves forward and looks at you closely. It says:

"I will help you. My name is [the dragon gives you their name.] You will need to study hard and meditate often so that our mental bonds grow tighter."

You thank the dragon and go back to the gate. The gate opens and all of you step through.

Instantly, you find yourself back inside your physical body. Move your fingers and feet slowly until you feel comfortable once more on the physical plane. The mediation is ended.

The first project your co-magician will have you do is to construct a pyramid. The pyramid can be made of paper, cardboard, or light copper sheets if you know a little soldering. Cardboard is not difficult to use. Just score the cardboard at each point where it needs to bend, and glue or tape it together at the tabbed side. If you wish, you can paint it.

On a small piece of paper, write down three things you want to appear in your life. Put the paper under the pyramid. As your requests get answered, cross them off the list. Also do a candle spell for at least one of your desires to help it manifest faster. Examples of candle spells are given in chapter 8.

I suggest starting with small desires so you can build up your confidence as they manifest. Some desires take much thought, preparation, and magickal procedure before they can happen. Magick takes patience and practice. Don't get discouraged.

SIX

MAGICK AND
THE PSYCHIC

When you work to enhance psychic abilities, eventually you begin using parts of the brain not used before. This may result in headaches or a sense of tightness between and just above the eyebrows. Once new neuro pathways are activated, they don't stay static but instead grow stronger and branch out. Magick and the psychic grow together in strength.

All magick is the gathering and solidifying of empowering energy for a specific purpose. You must make certain, as with weather-working, that the spell doesn't cause harm in unforeseen ways.

Magick is but a tool. Will, discipline, visualization, intent, and determination are the powers behind magick. Magick manifests itself in uncounted ways, many of which seem to surprise us. The way magick manifests a spell may be in an unexpected manner. The fact that it manifests at all should give you a feeling of confidence.

All things in the universe, and in nature itself, survive on the razor's edge that separates harmony and chaos. This is why magick works when you have practiced it enough. Learning how to place your intent and willpower at just the right point for proper pressure manifests magick.

The way each person works magick leaves signatures that are as individual as fingerprints. All magicians, even dragons, either individually or in a clan, have a similar personal signature.

The human consciousness, subconscious, and super-consciousness are substances outside the confines of the human body; they are a highly ordered energy capable of changing the physical world. Indeed, the mass effects of human minds can be measured on Random Event Generators. After 9/11, the Princeton Engineering Anomalies Research Lab in California found this startling evidence of human minds on thirty-seven Random Event Generators around the world. This can bring order out of chaos, thus paralleling the ancient spiritual belief of a cosmic consciousness, that human intent is capable of interacting with physical matter. Mass meditations and prayers produce similar events in Random Event Generators.

The conscious, subconscious, and super-conscious, according to Freud, are not parts of the human body or mind but of another dimension. The conscious is the one we are most aware of, as it is with us constantly to help guide us through life. The subconscious affects the body and mind according to what it has experienced through the consciousness, and it can even cause physical ailments and/or mental issues, whether of this life or a past life. The super-conscious is the great mind that is connected to everyone who has ever lived, to all cultures, and everything in the history of this world.

The art of magick in all its forms has been practiced and studied for thousands of years. If magick didn't work, if tangible results weren't seen, humans would have given up on it centuries ago. But we are still learning about magick and new (to us) methods of making it more efficient and productive. Somehow, dragons and magick seem to go together. The dragons themselves are magickal creatures but the connection goes beyond that—dragons are masters in using magick.

Knowledge equals energy equals matter equals mass. Mass distorts space which creates manifestation. This is the dragons' way of explaining magick and how it works. Humans recognize the statement as a scientific statement. Both descriptions are correct.

The dreaming states or deep meditation are the only states in which our psychic senses interact freely with our other five senses without distinction. When we dream, our natural ability to distinguish between the normal and the paranormal also disappears. Like with so many subjects, the more you learn about it, the more interesting it becomes.

During the dreaming state, the mind is free to work on a problem with both psychic and normal senses in a unique and extremely creative manner that can't be duplicated in the waking state. These two senses operate separately during waking hours so we can maneuver safely. So many things are invisible to us when we are awake.

Names have psychic power. Throughout history, many cultures believed in this power, such that if another person didn't know someone's secret (middle) name, no curse could be laid. That is why so many practitioners take a secret name for working with magick. To tell another one's secret magickal name is to give a part of one's identity—thereafter, the receiver has a form of power over the giver.

In a magickal attack, sometimes with great caution, you can "ride the beam" back to the sender and block it. However, it is much safer to use mirror or protection spells. The first thing you must do if you think you are under attack is to make certain it is true. If you are projecting negative thoughts about situations or other people, you may be attracting negative energies to yourself. If you are the recipient of a string of bad luck and are not guilty of dwelling on the negative, you can be certain you are at least under ill-wishing from someone. Most of the time, such streams of bad luck can be easily handled with a simple spell that does a "return to sender" action. See chapter 8 for examples.

A magician must learn how to put limits upon spells to keep them from manifesting in unwanted ways. First, be careful to work out the boundaries of the field of the spell; that is, exactly what the spell is to do. Then you need to determine the spell's duration. Things wear away in time, yet some residue will remain; you want to make certain this doesn't happen, that when its time is done, it is absorbed back into the astral. Since all spells work best when they are done according to the planets, phases of the moon, and such, you want to use these when casting the spell. You also need to think about the extent of the spell—do you want it to affect the family, friends, or people around you, or another person? Last, but certainly not least, you want to make sure that if the spell rebounds for whatever reason, you and yours will not be harmed; that the spell is dissipated into the earth. This is especially important if you finished the spell with the Charm of Making (chapter 8).

Spells and rituals are arranged according to their special powers, special correspondences, moon phases, yearly phases, and planetary combinations. Art is connected with rituals and spells, as well as in dragon healing. Thus, the use of carved symbols and sigils, or the drawing of the same on paper, will intensify the concentration and raise the astral power level for stronger spellcasting.

Because of the thousands of years of power being raised on the solstices, equinoxes, eclipses, and phases of the moon, these particular dates have become powerful in themselves on this earth plane. For example, if there are two full moons in a month, the second one is a blue moon, and has twice as much power for increasing spells. If there are two new moons in a month, the second one is called a black moon; it gives it twice as much energy for spells intended to decrease something. Eclipses affect spells according to the zodiac sign in which they happen. Effects of the solar eclipses last the longest, though keep in mind that the chance of them being a total eclipse directly over you is quite rare. Eclipses either balance or decrease things in your life, depending upon what is happening with you.

Solstices and equinoxes are neither positive nor negative—simply, they symbolize the progression of life through the year. The Spring Equinox in April is good for planting ideas or making plans that will take time to come to fruition. The summer solstice in June is for working on those ideas and plans. The Autumn Equinox in September is a harvest period, and the winter solstice in December is a resting period, where one reforms plans that didn't go as desired or works on ideas and plans to begin at the next Spring Equinox.

Runes, symbols, and sigils have names, shapes, and attributes. They are constellations of forces that cluster on each separate symbol. A single sigil, properly made with the appropriate words and thoughts, can draw its attributes to itself and surround itself with them. See chapter 5 and the Appendix for more on this.

Whatever energy we put out into the universe, good or bad, stays connected to us for a time. It is like there is an invisible thread attached to it. Eventually, it comes back and there is no way to know what else it will pick upon along the way. There is no way to know what, if anything, will get entangled in the string. Wearing proper protective stones keeps negative energies away from you.

Energy is energy, whether it takes a normal or psychic form. Using an intense amount of it gives you a rush if you do it wrong, but later you pay the price in exhaustion. This also can happen when you are a new practitioner.

A lot of humans are incapable of detecting preternatural visual markers, almost like color blindness. However, just because you can't see ultraviolet light doesn't mean it isn't there. For magickal purposes, one must do meditation and learn to shift mental modes to detect psychic happenings.

Some of the universal levels near ours do a kind of wobbly orbital dance. They are not all close enough at times for passage from ours to theirs. When one such level rarely gets near enough to us, there are a lot of sightings of UFOs, spirits, and other phenomena.

Practitioners of magick and meditation know things don't happen instantaneously; time and energy are required to prepare and then perform. Self-discipline, visualization, patience, and perseverance are valuable traits to cultivate that allow you to be the director—not the victim—of your life events.

In order to work magick, you have to trick part of your brain into cooperating. The right brain tries to ignore all linear rules because this half of the brain sees reality and possibility in terms of the infinite, a concept the left brain cannot conceive of as real. To the right brain, there is no such thing as time. To the left brain, everything runs on time. Whatever can't be seen by the human eyes, touched, tasted, or trapped in a laboratory container cannot possibly be real, the left brain tells us. Yet it cannot explain certain things that happen, no matter how hard it tries.

Magicians worldwide know the value of befriending a dragon and getting it to add energy to the spells. In fact, a willing dragon as a co-magician in magick can triple the human magician's creative power before spellwork even starts. If the human magician cements a bond with a co-magician dragon in a positive way—as equal partners—each is able to contribute a different ingredient to the work and spells begin to manifest faster.

Even if you have heard of nothing else about astrology other than your zodiac sign, you have likely heard about Mercury retrograde, the mayhem dispenser of Murphy's Law. Three to four times a year, for about three to four weeks at a time, the planet Mercury appears to move in reverse when compared to Earth. Other planets also go retrograde, but none of them produce the uncertainty and chaos that Mercury does.

Little Mercury affects such vital life features as computers, telephones—indeed, any electronic or technological device. Messages, packages, mailed payments, and especially e-mails disappear into the Multiverse, never to be seen again. Files may vaporize in your computer, if the entire system doesn't crash, leaving you to reinstall everything. Communications are a quarter turn off with nearly everyone. In some ways, it is like the Huns suddenly ride into town! Mercury retrograde affects each zodiac sign differently, especially the signs through which it moves, so you need to be especially careful how you word spells and be extra cautious about using your will and intent should you cast during this retrograde event.

You will find that the more you use magick, the stronger and more accurate the psychic side of your nature becomes. The two attributes strengthen and balance each other.

SEVEN

PREPARATION FOR
DRAGON MAGICK

Dragons and humans appear to have more in common than one would think. Dragons hold honor, truth, spiritual paths, and generally living a good life in as high regard as we do. We may not exactly see many things in the same way, but we seem to reach the same conclusions. The more we interact with each other, the closer we become as partners in work on all levels, but especially with magick. That is a wonderful thing!

To perform magick on all levels and thereby balance yourself and your life, you need to work on yourself mentally and spiritually, as well as on your physical and material wishes. Even dragons know the importance of the spiritual, although I have never learned anything about how they personally view spiritual matters, except as being part of the Great Source. Above all, remember that each dragon has an individual character with emotions, actions and reactions, and likes and dislikes. The type of clan can have an influence on this as well, and care should be taken if you want to work with certain clans: they can be tricky with answers, mislead you, or ignore you altogether. Part of the discernment you need to learn is being able to see through this kind of deception, as these clans simply don't trust or like humans. Overall, it is best to rely on your guardian dragon and your co-magician.

The focus of all-being, the innermost truth or essence of something, is what magicians call the true name of that being: understanding that is the key to magick, and the ability to discern it is the mark of a true magician. The consequences of our actions are always so complicated, so diverse, that predicting the future is a very difficult business. The first subject to understand is yourself.

In preparation for learning about the elements, you need to realize that you will gain little unless you employ all your senses: sight, touch, taste, hearing, feeling, and smell. When you can use your senses and they are providing information back to you, you are well on your way to doing productive magick.

SEASONAL MEDITATION

In preparation for meditation, choose a time and place where you will not be disturbed.

While in the meditation, you will not be aware of time, and you are unlikely to be fully aware of what is happening around you unless the mind senses danger, in which case you will be able to return to your body at once. The same applies if you are fearful of anything you see during this time. You are never trapped, caught, in danger of losing your soul, or whatever else people fear; you can open your eyes any time and be back in normal time and place.

Sit in your chair with your feet flat on the floor with your hands in your lap. Take slow, deep breaths, relaxing more of your body's muscles each time. Visualize yourself surrounded by brilliant white light, with your guardian spirits at your side. Your body relaxes more and more until you feel light and very comfortable. Feel yourself standing beside a well. If anything or anyone in life is upsetting you, drop it or them into the well. They fall down into the darkness away from you. Walk away from the well, leaving every annoying person and event behind.

You and your guardian are standing in a hall facing four doors. You open the door marked Spring and step through. You see trees in bloom or showing new leaf buds. A few early flowers are blossoming along a path, filling the air with a mild, sweet scent. You reach out to touch the soft fuzzy catkins on a pussy willow. You and your guardian explore for a few more minutes, then go back through the door.

As you shut the Spring door, the entrance to Summer opens. You step through into a sunny, warm meadow. It is covered in long grass and wildflowers. Birds are everywhere. You hear crickets in the shade of trees. You continue to explore for several minutes, noticing the difference between spring and summer. Then you and your guardian go back through the door.

As you step through, you see a flurry of bright autumn leaves blowing through Autumn's door. You step through to see a field of colorful pumpkins decorated with scarecrows. The air is crisp; the moon full and bright overhead. A pint of cider is sitting on a stump in the pumpkin patch; you taste it and find it has a pleasant crisp flavor. After exploring for a time, you go back through the door.

The door marked Winter is open. A shower of snowflakes floats in on a gust of chilly air. You visualize a coat and hat, which you put on against the cold. Ahead of you is a street lined with decorated trees. The reflected colored lights glow on the snow. Several houses are decorated also. You feel the happiness in the air, happiness that will soon grow into the new year. You hear church chimes and far off singing by a group of carolers. You and your guardian wander around a bit before going back through the door.

Instantly, you find yourself back inside your physical body. Move your fingers and feet slowly until you feel comfortable once more on the physical plane. The mediation is ended.

⊙   ⊙   ⊙

Now is the time to think about what you experienced in each season. What were your feelings about each one? Were you using all your senses? Think back to your other meditations. Are your senses coming through better than when you started? To become a proficient magician, one must strengthen the senses on both the physical and the astral realms. This is necessary for both manifestation of spells and protecting yourself.

Earth, air, fire, and water are natural forces. In spellwork, it is not the elements that are unnatural but the way in which they are combined. To achieve an end, it is sufficient just to shift the balance of the natural order, to distort the present pattern, just for a little while. The forces of manifestation do not need to send things to a special effects studio to achieve their ends.

If the seasons begin to fluctuate too much out of the cycles, the dragons of the seasons must determine the cause and take action in tandem with the elemental dragons to rectify the seasons. The weather dragons also help.

Elements

Most magicians are aware of the usual four elements that are required to perform magick and make it work properly. Traditionally, they are earth, air, fire, and water. The dragons have six elements, however: earth, air, fire, water, storm, and spirit (or as they call it, eye of the dragon). Look at the sigils for these elements carefully before you do the meditation. You might want to copy them, trim them to their circular size, and paste them on thin cardboard. Whenever you do rituals, you can then set these sigils in the proper directions to make your magick more powerful. Consider using a compass to make certain the directions are correct. We often think we know where north is, for instance, but we can be a quarter turn off.

The air element is ruled by the dragon Sairys, is pure yellow, and is associated the eastern direction. It works with any type of air movement as well as any project dealing with the mental realm.

Fire is ruled by Fafnir, is pure red, and is associated with the south. Besides physical fire, this element affects all physical action, changes, and willpower. It also can be used when working on spiritual action, such as self changes within.

Water is ruled by the dragon Naelyon, is blue, and is associated with the west. It works with the emotional realm as well as all water from tiny ponds to the oceans.

Earth is a solid element ruled by Grael. It is dark green, represents the north, and is the realm of physical matter, including the body.

The planet Earth has an electromagnetic energy field (an aura), just as humans do. This field is composed of various strengths of elemental energy in both positive and negative flows. When all four elements are empowered at one time and balanced with earth, this energy transforms into a dynamic manifesting force called storm.

The storm element, guarded by the Storm-Bringer clan led by Charoesia, is far stronger than the four elements plus spirit. If you work with stones associated with storm, they create massive transformations and cleaning, radical shifts in life. Use these stones for only short periods of time and only when you're ready for such massive changes in your internal and external worlds.

Storm is an element it is best not to form artificially, but rather to allow to coalesce by itself. This element is a link or bridge to the void of the chaos dragons, which chaos dragons both destroy and create, or, in this case, recreate as part of an energy pattern. Storm comes into action when a being's life path or the direction of a planet or galaxy's future goes off course. With humans, this usually happens when the person goes through what is called "the dark night of the soul." The person knows drastic changes are essential but sees no solutions. It is here the Storm-Bringers step in, taking decisions out of the person's hand and control. But when the clouds lift and the lightning stops, those who go through such a period in life find themselves and their direction in life changed in a manner they never expected, changed only if they accept the cleansing. The storm element works on one rule: accept the transformation, work with it, and become stronger or be destroyed by it.

The only way to really grasp the essentials of the working of elements is to experience each one through a deep meditation. This type of meditation engages all the senses, which you still have and can use when traveling in the Otherworld. Your sense on this level will be stronger, brighter, and sharper than those of this physical plane.

ELEMENT MEDITATION

In preparation for meditation, choose a time and place where you will not be disturbed. While in the meditation, you will not be aware of time, and you are unlikely to be fully aware of what is happening around you unless the mind senses danger, in which case you will be able to return to your body at once. The same applies if you are fearful of anything you see during this time. You are never trapped, caught, in danger of losing your soul, or whatever else people fear; you can open your eyes any time and be back in normal time and place.

Sit in your chair with your feet flat on the floor with your hands in your lap. Take slow, deep breaths, relaxing more of your body's muscles each time. Visualize yourself surrounded by brilliant white light with your guardian spirits at your side. Your body relaxes more and more until you feel light and very comfortable. Feel yourself standing beside a well. If anything or anyone in life is upsetting you, drop it or them into the well. They fall down into the darkness away from you. Walk away from the well, leaving every annoying person and event behind.

You are standing on a hilltop next to your co-magician dragon. A crisp breeze blows around you, sweeping into the small valley just beyond. You slowly become aware that the breeze is blowing through you as well as around you. You hear soft voices and sounds, many of them carried from the other side of the Earth. Any noise made anywhere around the globe remains in the jet stream until it finally fades away. You see the individual air molecules bump together as they speed past. You can taste the sharp ozone of an approaching storm as those molecules rasp against your skin. Your dragon leaps into the breeze, riding the currents leisurely.

You release the idea that you can't fly and let the breeze carry you far above the hilltop. You swoop down toward the valley with your dragon, moving just above the trees, savoring the freedom this event gives you. Your mind opens to the freshness of ideas, letting the cobwebs blow away.

You look down to find you have quickly moved out over the ocean. Foam-capped waves roll toward the sandy beach, leaving behind driftwood and shells as they withdraw. Your dragon reassures you that being underwater will not harm you, as they dive deep into the ocean below. You follow and the dragon speaks to the fish that swirl around you as you pass. You feel the delicate but rough-textured touch of a fin against your arm. As when in the air, you discover that sounds carry a long way through the water. The chatter of dolphins gets closer until several of them are swimming alongside, their funny smiles drawing your smile in return. Your emotional realm feels calm and washed clean. As the dolphins leap above the ocean surface in their lively dance, you too surface and see the red of hot lava and the wall of steam just ahead, where an active volcano joins the ocean.

"Don't be afraid," your dragon says. "You can't be harmed." The dragon soars straight toward the volcano and lands close beside the glowing lava stream.

As soon as your feet touch the ground beside your dragon, you become aware of many sensations you haven't experienced before. You see small firedrakes moving freely in and out of the lava. You reach in and one climbs into your hand. The two of you look at each other for a few moments before the small dragon leaps back into the hot lava. You realize you felt only a slight warmth and the prickle of tiny claws when you held the firedrake. The lava hisses and crackles where it meets the cold of the water, sending a burning smell into the air. The energy of fire begins to course through your astral body, filling you to overflowing with a desire to move, to be active.

As you and your dragon fly away from the volcano toward a lush tropical forest, you realize you need the grounding of the element of earth. Your astral body has absorbed an imbalance of air, water, and fire. You dive straight down at the ground, entering the earth without a sound and without a sign left behind of your entrance. You flip over to lie on your back, your arms spread wide in the soft soil. You hear small noises made by creatures who inhabit the ground, but none near you. Each intake of breath fills your senses with a rich odor of dirt and the scent of flowers. You relax and take in needed earth energy to balance you. You hear your dragon sigh with pleasure as they also soak up earth power. Your astral body comes back into balance.

You pop out of the ground to stand beside your co-magician dragon. You see a small double vortex hanging in the air above the tropical forest. Your dragon explains that you are seeing a small example of the storm element, an energy field that moves both clockwise and counterclockwise at the same time. This element is used to create massive changes in all things. At any future time, when you feel this type of change is necessary, you can enter the storm element.

You look up at the sky and see a huge dragon eye. It is gold and black against a white crystalline-skin background. You realize that this is the dragons' representation of spirit—the eye of the dragon. You throw your arms wide in thanks for experiencing the elements.

Instantly, you find yourself back inside your physical body. Move your fingers and feet slowly until you feel comfortable once more on the physical plane. The mediation is ended.

◎   ◎   ◎

Note that in this meditation, I didn't take you into the storm element. The reason is that entering it is a very personal decision and really does create transformation. The magician is only able when they are ready for that experience. When necessary, the Chaos dragons will introduce you to that element, and it will definitely happen more than once. I've discovered that their insight into my experience of storm is better than mine, so I wait.

Vibrational Energy

Now that you are more familiar with the elements, you should be much more aware of everything around you, including astral vibrations. You will be sensitive to thought-forms, for example, and be able to tell if they are positive or negative.

Thought-forms have the ability to become little spirits if enough of them meld together with the same type of energy, positive or negative. The malevolent ones can move like a cloud of drifting dust; some accumulate in old and newer houses or buildings. They can affect humans and pets as well. If these types of energies are directed toward a certain person, they can disrupt the life pattern flow and affect the health of body, mind, spirit—what we would call luck. This disruption used to be called ill-wishing or the evil eye. In truth, the consequences of our actions are always so complicated and diverse that predicting the future is a very difficult business. We simply know when things are suddenly going wrong and need to do something about it. The remedy may be as simple as hanging a mirror to face the house's main door. Clean the mirror monthly and say: "Mirror shield, where you are set, capture all evils and ill seeds, return them to the senders and negate their deeds. As I say, so shall it be."

A psychic nasty is a negative energy form that exists outside of the realm in which we live. It has never lived on Earth. An ordinary protection amulet protects us from a human attacker but not a psychic nasty. Most of the time when you unwittingly come across such an entity, its energy isn't strong enough to firmly attach to you. It may follow and keep circling it you until finds a chink in your psychic shield so it can slip through. In the process it drains as much of your energy as it can. Anyone aware of this and doing a negative spell or ill-wishing can use the bad energy to give the spell a little extra punch. However, you have to word the spell in such a way that the negative energy doesn't rebound. Wearing or carrying hematite (that absorbs negativity) and fire agate (that returns the negativity to the sender) are both helpful.

Oftentimes what we pick up on has to do with problems within our auras and chakras. Each person has many layers of auras surrounding their body, and far more chakras than the well-known seven. These need to be cleansed periodically. In fact, it is a good practice to do a smudging or cleansing with sage or frankincense and myrrh incense on a monthly basis. Slowly sweep the burning incense stick carefully and slowly up the back and front of your body while visualizing your auras and chakras all radiating with freshness.

As a dragon magician, you can invoke more travel energy by mentally walking a spiral path to invoke dragon breath energy in the earth's astral body. Each spiral lifts you into the astral and the special place where the Dragon Council will meet. Physically walking a spiral or labyrinth, tracing the lines of a hand-held model, or mentally walking the spiral changes your brain waves and creates an altered state of consciousness, especially just prior to entering a meditation.

SPIRAL PATH TO
UPPERWORLD MEDITATION

In preparation for meditation, choose a time and place where you will not be disturbed. While in the meditation, you will not be aware of time, and you are unlikely to be fully aware of what is happening around you unless the mind senses danger, in which case you will be able to return to your body at once. The same applies if you are fearful of anything you see during this time. You are never trapped, caught, in danger of losing your soul, or whatever else people fear; you can open your eyes any time and be back in normal time and place.

You find yourself in a small crowd of beings standing a short distance from the golden gate to the Highests. Directly in front of the gate are several large older dragons who are communicating with the goddess, the god, and the old dragon (called She Who Dwells Within the Greatest) just beyond the gate. Though you can hear the voices, nothing said makes any sense to you. What discussion you can pick up on seems to be about the routine and various happenings throughout the Multiverse, and the fact that the cloud entity known as the Annihilator has not appeared for some time.

Suddenly, you feel the gaze of the oldest dragon beyond the gate. You look straight into her eyes and know nothing in your life is hidden from her. You know her name is Kaudra and that she is keeper of the crystal cave, and you feel an urge to go to her and ask if she will let you enter. Your co-magician dragon appears at your side and nods in agreement. The two of you walk toward Kaudra, who uncurls and yawns widely. You feel her warm greetings within your mind.

"You must enter alone," your dragon tells you. "If you ask for advice, you will be told what you need, not what you want. If you are not open to such truth yet, sit a while in one of the shrine areas and think upon your life and goals. Return here when finished, and I will escort you to a dragon healing session."

You enter the shadowy cave entrance to find yourself inside a huge geode lined with crystals of every kind and color. Straight ahead is the crystal bubble of the dream chamber. You bypass this and wander down a hall, looking into side chambers that contain meditation seats, ledge-beds, counselor benches, thrones with smaller seats, and small shrines. You enter one throne chamber and find the god or goddess sitting on a throne, waiting to talk to you. Angels stand beside the throne. You sit on the smaller seat and listen to the spiritual messages given to you.

The deity finishes and disappears. You walk back outside and follow your dragon to the Temple of All-Healing. The temple sits within the Garden of Wisdom and Solitude, where a high hedge encloses an endless garden of all Earth's botanical cultures and some from other galaxies. This garden is filled with a multitude of shrines, temples, gazebos, and flower-covered shelters. The flower-lined paths lead you past small streams, waterfalls, fountains, ponds, and over short bridges.

The Temple of All-Healing is a massive white marble building with room after room of tables covered with richly embroidered blankets. Dragons and angels are working over many people already on the healing tables. Your dragon leads you to an empty table where a dragon patiently waits.

You lie down on the table, close your eyes, and relax. You hear beautiful music and smell the flowers from the garden outside. As the healer moves her hands slowly over you, touching and adjusting a place here and there, you relax even more under the current of warm loving energy as it flows through you on its healing mission.

When the healer finishes, you thank her and go with your dragon back out into the great garden.

Instantly, you find yourself back inside your physical body. Move your fingers and feet slowly until you feel comfortable once more on the physical plane. The mediation is ended.

EIGHT

BASIC RITUALS

The very first part of ritual should be learning to meditate. This discipline not only teaches you the strength in silence but also grooms you for the importance of visualization and intent, which are so necessary for strong, productive spells. It also is valuable practice for working with your co-magician dragon.

The magician must learn to practice meditation at least on a regular basis for it to be helpful. Meditation stimulates the psychic centers and teaches self-discipline and patience. Every magician also must learn and practice silence. Silence, in this sense, means that you do not talk about the magickal rituals you are performing. The only exception I know is if you are working with a like-minded individual or group; even then, talk about the work should be kept to a minimum so as not to drain off the energy put into the spell or ritual.

One important fact to remember whenever you do any magick is that it is definitely *not* a game. If you plan to only dabble in magick, I strongly suggest you forget trying dragon rituals. Stick to simple candle-burning spells without any backing to them. Dragon power and elemental type energies are not something to play around with and are only for the serious magician. Simply playing at dragon magick can invite terrific negative backlash. Dragons are not noted for being cooperative or patient with insincere magick practitioners; like other types of powerful spiritual and astral entities, dragons will quickly weed out the dedicated from the casually interested.

If you are sincere about advancing your skills as a magician, I heartily wish you well. Becoming acquainted with dragon power is an extremely satisfying experience.

I have already given you several meditations you may use for preparing to do rituals. Rather than try to remember them, you can record them onto an audiotape and play them during your mediation times. Remember, you are always able to leave a meditation whenever you wish; you will *not* lose your soul, no matter what someone tells you. That said, note that when your meditation runs deep, someone or something touching or talking to you will make you feel as if you have been shocked. You may be so startled that it may take you several minutes to get your breathing and mind to function properly again.

FULL FORMAL RITUAL

First, I will give you an example of a full formal ritual with calling the elements and such. If possible, you should at least do this ritual on the solstices, equinoxes, and new and full moons. The positive benefits to that of your home and your energy are powerful.

What follows is the basis of all formal dragon rituals. The magician can insert her/his own creations, such as music, dance, meditation, or small pieces of self-written ritual in appropriate places without disrupting the flow of energy. As you can see by reading through this ceremony, certain things need to be done at certain times. Beyond that, the magician can do what feels right personally.

Gather everything you will need inside your ritual area and make what preparations you can to not be disturbed. For the altar, a plaque of a five-pointed star within a circle can be kept to symbolize the balance of elements. One point is kept pointing upward to symbolize the dragons of light and dark, as they rule over all the elemental kingdoms. An image or statuary of a dragon clutching such a star is also helpful. You will also need a chalice of water, black and white candles (one each), a small dish of salt, and a wand.

If you are performing magick to lessen or decrease something, in any place that says "circle clockwise," you should circle counterclockwise.

Set the altar in the center facing the east, since that will be your beginning and ending points. Light a white candle at one end of the altar and a black candle at the other end. Begin the ritual by "drawing" your magickal circle clockwise on the floor with your wand while saying:

By dragon power, this circle is sealed.

Return to the altar. Point the wand at the dragon pentagram and say:

Dragons of spirit, highest of dragons and
most powerful, bless this altar with your
fire. Let us be one in magick, o dragons
great and wise.

Set the water chalice on the pentacle. Circle the chalice three times clockwise with the wand and say:

Air, Fire, Earth, bring power forth.
Water of land and sea, purified be.

Hold the chalice high; say:

Draconis! Draconis! Draconis!

Sprinkle the water lightly around the circled area, beginning and ending in the east.

Set the dish of salt on the pentacle. Circle it three times clockwise and say:

Water, Air, Fire, hear my desire.
Salt of earth and sea, purified be.

Sprinkle a few grains of salt to each corner of the altar. Circle the incense and any herbs three times clockwise and say:

Incense magickal, incense bold,
Awaken the dragons, as of old.
I call you purified.
Draconis! Draconis! Draconis!

Light the incense and carry it around the circled area, beginning and ending in the east. Return it to the altar.

Stand before the altar, wand in hand, and mentally dedicate yourself to the study of dragon magick. Project your interest and love of dragons as strongly as you can. Say:

Arise, O breath of dragons.
Fill this place with goodness.
Bless me and mine with
your positive energies,
And repel all those who
wish us harm in any form.
I welcome all dragons who
come to this place of power.
May we work in harmony
and in love.
May this sacred spot become
a haven of centered-ness.
A refuge that revitalizes. A door
that leads to Otherworld knowledge.

May your powers become one with mine.
That I, my family, my community,
my country, the world,
May become whole and healthy again.
Powers of Water, Earth, Fire, and Skies.

Then point the wand at the dragon pentacle and say:

Behold, all dragons and rulers of dragons,
I am (magickal name), a magician
who seeks dragon magick.
With wand in my hand,
I enter the realms of the dragons.
Not for physical battle,
but for knowledge and power.
I greet you, O dragons ancient and wise,
And await your blessing and guidance.

Still holding the wand in your power hand, take the pentacle in your other hand and face the east. Point the want and hold up the pentacle facing outward. Draw an invoking pentagram (start at the topmost point and draw the star shape clockwise) with the wand. Say:

From Sairys, ruler of the
eastern dragons fair,
Comes now the wondrous
power of air.

Turn now to the south. Again, use the wand to draw the invoking pentagram, and hold up the pentacle. Say:

From Fafnir, ruler of dragons of the south,
Comes cleansing fire from dragon mouth.

Turn to the west. Again, use the wand to draw the invoking pentagram, and hold up the pentacle. Say:

From Naelyan, ruler of
dragons of the west,
Comes the power of water,
three times blessed.

Turn to the north. Again, use the wand to draw the invoking pentagram, and hold up the pentacle. Say:

> *From Grael, ruler of dragons of the north,*
> *The power of earth does now come forth.*

(At this point in your ritual, insert the proper chants and works for the particular spellworking you have chosen.) When finished, tap the altar three times and chant:

> *I thank you, dragons old and wise,*
> *Of Earth and Fire, Water, Skies,*
> *For sharing wisdom here with me*
> *As we will, so shall it be.*

To end the ritual, take the wand and draw a banishing pentagram (draw a star figure starting at the lower left point and draw clockwise) in the east. Say:

> *Go in peace, dragons of the east.*
> *And return again in the ritual hour.*

Take the wand and turn to the south. Draw the banishing pentagram and say:

Go in peace, dragons of the south
And return again in the ritual hour.

Take the wand and go to the west. Draw the banishing pentagram and say:

Go in peace, dragons of the west.
And return again in the ritual hour.

Take the wand and turn to to the north. Draw the banishing pentagram and say:

Go in peace, dragons of the north.
And return again in the ritual hour.

Return to the altar. Raise both arms and say:

Farewell to you, o dragons fair,
Fire, Water, Earth, and Air.
Together we make magick well
By power deep and dragon spell.
In peace go now. Return once more
To teach me magick and ancient lore.
Draconis! Draconis! Draconis!

Cut the circle with a backward sweep of the wand across the boundary line. Extinguish the altars. Clear the altar of all tools, except any spell-related candles you have lit.

CANDLE-BURNING RITUALS

If you know how to properly do a candle-burning spell, it can be quite productive. Each oil and herb you put on the candle, each sigil or symbol you carve into it with concentrated intent, gives it more power to be released when the candle is burned. I prefer votive candles for such spells because they can be safely left in a cauldron to burn completely out. To more easily remove the wax leftover (and there usually is some), coat the inside bottom of the cauldron with a little cooking oil. This saves you from having to dig and scrape. Never burn a candle on top of previous wax. Not only will the spells become confused, but you could run the risk of starting a fire.

You can either use the oil suggested with each spell or make your own special blends. Following are several blends you may want to make, label, and keep on your altar for occasions when you are in a hurry.

Mystic Oil

Put a half teaspoon of almond oil into a one-ounce vial with a cap. Slowly add one drop each of cinnamon and clove oils. Add five to seven drops of sandalwood oil and five drops of myrrh oil. Close the vial tightly and hold it between your hands. Chant:

> *Mystic oil of spiritual light,*
> *Make my magick clear and bright.*
> *Fill my candles with strong power,*
> *Whenever I call a ritual hour.*

Protection/Defense Oil

Put a half teaspoon of almond oil into a one-ounce vial with a cap. Slowly add one drop of cedar oil, one drop of bay oil, and six drops of frankincense oil. Hold it between your hands and chant:

Defend me (us) from all chaos and ill will.
Put solid boundary around me (us) until
The danger stops and harmony is clear.
Ill-wishing has no place here.

Prosperity Oil

Put a half teaspoon of almond oil into a one-ounce vial with a cap. Slowly add five drops of High John the Conqueror oil, three drops of cinnamon oil, and eight drops of bergamot oil. Hold it between your hands and chant:

Money green and silver bright,
I call to you, which is my right.

These sample candle-burning spells can be used alone or as part of a more formal ritual as given above. All you will need are: a small knife, small amounts of herbs and oils, a paper towel, a safe candleholder to allow the candle to burn out, and your wand.

Begin by carving any symbol you have chosen into the candle. (See the Appendix for a wide choice of symbols, remembering to use the proper day and hour to really give your spell a punch of power.)

Holding the votive in both hands, breathe your intent onto the candle. Then crush the herbs into small pieces. It will only take a half to one teaspoonful of the mixed herbs per votive candle; half a teaspoon is usually more than enough. Spread the herbs in a thin layer on the paper towel. Put a drop or two of oil in the palm of one hand and, turning the candle clockwise, oil the candle from top to bottom by turning it in your hand. This is for positive spells; turn the candle counterclockwise for defense spells. Then roll it in the herbs on the paper towel. The towel is also handy to wipe the remaining oil from your hands.

Light the votive and chant the spell.

Place the candle in the holder in a safe place; it is best to leave it to burn out completely. Circle the candle clockwise with your wand three times and say:

> Let this spell continue on,
> From day to day and sun to sun,
> Until its intent is well begun,
> Or I end its run.
> If this spell should negatively rebound,
> Send its energy into the ground.
> If so, dissolve its intent and energy
> Protect me and mine. So mote it be.

Light the candle and place the stone in front of the candle to aid the energy flow.

The next day, dispose of any remaining wax and clean your altar space.

Love Spell
Needed: Pink candle, jasmine oil, dried rose petals, ginger power, a lodestone.

> *True love is missing from my life,*
> *Causing loneliness and strife.*
> *Fill this gap with happiness,*
> *So with this love I may be blessed.*

True Love Spell
Needed: Pink candle, jasmine or rose oil, crushed rose petals. This spell is best done at a full moon or on a Friday during the hour of Venus.

> *Only true love enters here.*
> *I see all truth and have no fear.*
> *My heart is open and awake,*
> *To right choices I shall make.*
> *Heart to heart, one to one,*
> *My search for true love soon is done.*
> *So must it be!*

Money and Prosperity

Needed: Green candle, bergamot or honeysuckle oil, cinnamon powder, pine needles, fir needles, and a lodestone or staurolite stone.

> *Financial burdens hold me back,*
> *From living life without lack.*
> *Money, money, come now to me.*
> *As I wish, to shall it be.*

Change My Luck Spell

Needed: Orange candle, lemon oil or lotus oil, frankincense powder, grated lemon rind or zest, and a lodestone.

> *My life's path is on a negative run.*
> *Please change this direction to a positive one.*
> *Bring me good luck and opportunity.*
> *That I may prosper. Let it be.*

Uncrossing Spell

Needed: Black candle, clove oil, myrrh powder, vervain powder, orris root power, petrified wood or tektite.

> *Remove the negative ties that bind*
> *And cause misfortune to me and mine.*
> *Fill me with light, not adversity,*
> *So I am free of ill-wishing. So mote it be.*

It will help to smudge your house with sage incense after you light this candle. You may also want to smudge your vehicles.

Anti-Hex Spell

Needed: One walnut shell broken at the seam and empty of walnut meat; black thread or thin cord; and cobwebs. Put the cobwebs inside the empty shell, then tie the two parts together with black thread. Say:

> *Your ill-wishing in this web is bound,*
> *And further tied up, round and round.*
> *I plant your evil in the earth,*
> *So its fulfillment has no birth!*
> *So shall it be!*

Bury the shell in the ground.

House Clearing Spell

Needed: White candles, cedar oil, crushed bay leaf, cinnamon powder, lavender buds, coral or quartz crystal.

> *Negatives have no place here:*
> *So room by room this dwelling I clear.*
> *Little dragons, eat your fill,*
> *Until only positive energy remains here.*

Smudge your house or apartment room by room, from the back rooms, working your way to the front door. You may feel the pressure of negativity being pushed before you until you open the front door and tell the intruders to get out.

For candle-burning spells, circle the candle three times clockwise for increasing magick, or three times counterclockwise for decreasing magick. Before lighting the candle, tap the dragon pentacle and say:

> *Come, Draconis.*
> *By your all-consuming breath,*
> *I summon you.*
> *By your piercing gaze, I summon you.*

By your mighty strength, I summon you.
By your wisdom ancient and cunning,
I summon you.
By your magick deep and old,
I summon you.
Come, Draconis, to my call!

Tap the candle lightly and say:

Draonis! Draconis! Draconis!
Hear my call.
Three times I call you. Listen all!
This candle's flame is like your fire.
Dragons, bring my heat's desire.
Dragon power, come to me.
Hear my words. So mote it be.
Draconis! Draconis! Draconis!

Light the candle and say the chant that goes with it. To end all rituals, and before cutting the circle, say the Charm of Making:

By glow of Sun, the power's begun.
By moonbeam's light, the spell is right.
To create desire by Earth and Fire,
Water, Air, make magick fair.
Powerful charm of making, creative
Magickal undertaking.
By Storm, be formed!

To astrally cleanse your house of negative vibrations, first physically clean it, then smudge it with dragon's blood resin incense. While smudging it, chant:

O great dragons, wondrous, wise.
All of Earth, Air, Water, Skies,
Light and Darkness, join me here
To sweep this space all clean and clear.
Away with evil, in with right,
Dragons of Darkness and of Light.
Elementals, strong and old,
Restore the balance, dragons bold.

The house should feel empty now, but you don't want to leave it that way. You want to fill it with Light. Chant:

Light calls to Light.
Only those of Light
may enter here.
The way is barred to all
those who wish me harm.
I give my greeting only
to the Light.

Finish by chanting:

Farewell to you, O dragons fair,
Fire, Water, Earth, and Air.
Together we make magick well,
By power deep and dragon spell.
In peace go now. Return once more
To teach me magick and ancient lore.
Draconis! Draconis! Draconis!

To Dissolve or Stop and Ground a Spell

You are responsible for whatever you create with spells. Sometimes things go wrong, or you can feel the spell energy flapping around wildly, causing problems you didn't intend. You need to dissolve and stop that spell before it causes more havoc. You also need to ground it so that the energy doesn't harm anyone, including you.

You will need both a magenta and a black candle, a metal bowl to contain burnt material, a piece of paper with the spell's intent written on it, and a long metal knife to lift the paper so it all burns.

Place the black candle in a holder to the back of your altar, the metal bowl with the spell's intent written on paper in the middle, and the magenta candle to the front of your altar.

Light the black candle and say:

> *This spell I sent returns to me.*
> *I stop its travel, three times three.*
> *Its power flows into the ground,*
> *that on me it won't rebound.*
> *Earth, Air, Water, Fire, dragons*
> *all, this is my desire.*
> *By Storm, it shall be done.*

Burn the paper in the metal bowl. Light the magenta candle and say:

> *Faster than a dragon's thought, this*
> *spell's Intent shall come to naught.*
> *Its desire and purpose I set free.*
> *This I do Want. So must it be.*

Traveling Magick Kit

Magick amulets, stones, or tools are quite useful, and there are many you can use for different purposes. What follows can be considered a magickal traveling first aid kit.

You will need: your favorite stone or series of stones to cover several possible needs, small cones of incense (and a safe burner), a calming perfume such as lavender to spritz your bed or the room, a small amount of sea salt, your journal to record dreams and experiences, one or two lucky charms, small tea light candles in colors that will match several magickal spells, and a small, short wand.

Except for perhaps your journal, keep your items in a box or container. You never know when you will need to work magick on an unexpected problem.

HIGH ELDERS MEDITATION

In preparation for meditation, choose a time and place where you will not be disturbed.

You will not be aware of time. Nor are you likely to be fully aware of what is happening around you, unless the mind senses dangers. In this case, you will be able to return to your body at once. The same applies if you are fearful of anything you see during this time. You are never trapped, caught, in danger of losing your soul, or whatever else people fear; you can open your eyes any time and be back in normal time and place.

You are in Kaudra's crystal-lined cave in the Upperworld. You co-magician dragon is with you. You have been granted permission to attend a meeting of the Duaar, composed of High Elders from all worlds on all levels of the Multiverse.

As all the gathered beings move into the cave and into the transparent crystal bubble there, you see sentient Elders from all over the Multiverse. There are also mythical beings—including elves, faeries, and angels, and some you don't recognize.

"This is called the Dream Chamber," your dragon whispers as the two of you enter behind the Elders and sit in an unobtrusive place.

"How do the members of the Duaar get chosen?" you whisper back.

"They are chosen because of their wisdom and the fact that none of them have ever been government or religious leaders. All follow freewill spiritual paths. They each work with a small group of people on their original world, trying to lead them to the Truth. They hope, in this way, to influence positive changes."

The Duaar discuss the growth pains affecting planets, including Earth, throughout the Multiverse: pandemics, war, physical violence, prejudice, religious clashes, diseases, declining ethics, hunger, and poverty, as well as the gradual loss of personal freedoms. Some members speak sadly of the conflict of living in balance with a planet and its environment. Similar troubles affect all the represented worlds.

A few planets in the Multiverse are sliding backward into chaotic social conditions, which threaten all levels of growth for sentient beings, particularly their options to yet correct the situation. None of the Council knows yet what the final outcome will be.

The first step is freedom of spiritual paths without organized religious organizations trying to impose each of their views on everyone else. It is almost a unanimous decision with the Duaar that a control-attitude by religious organizations and governments is responsible for both the chaotic and lackadaisical responses of a world's inhabitants.

Energies should be attuned more to population control and making changes for a happy, positive life. Each culture, race, country, and planet should care for itself and ask for help from others only when disaster hits. Invasions and war must end. No culture, race, country, or planet is as it was in the beginning, due to the movement of groups, natural disasters, and many poor choices made by religious and national leaders. It is therefore time to forget what happened in the past (except for the lessons learned) and go forward from this point. There never was, isn't now, and never will be "one path for everyone," whether one is speaking of government, spirituality, ways of thinking, or how anyone thinks about any particular subject.

"All on Earth are part of an automatic diversity, as it should be," says the Earth representative. "That fact should be realized as truth and accepted. This also applies to all planets on all levels of the Multiverse. The successful planets all accepted and applied these ideas by mutual consent, after experiencing thousands of years of violent history similar to that of Earth. In doing this, most of these planets pulled their very existence back from the brink of total disintegration."

Everyone nods in agreement, knowing this is the truth but realizing that they dare not impose this truth by force.

You feel the dragon Kaudra as she projects the image of strands of all possible futures onto the ceiling of the Dream Chamber.

"There are very few events that cannot be changed." Kaudra's telepathic voice is heard by all. "You can only try."

You watch the Duaar as they send positive energy currents from the tips of their fingers to influence mergers of strands, and as they try to weave strands with their hands and minds.

Quietly, so you don't disturb their concentration, you leave the meeting. However, you do have renewed hope for Earth and a greater understanding of the heavy duties of members of the Duaar.

Instantly, you find yourself back inside your physical body. Move your fingers and feet slowly until you feel comfortable once more on the physical plane. The mediation is ended.

N|N E

THE FIRST CLANS TO
RETURN TO THIS PLANE

I wrote about the first clans in *Mystical Dragon Magick*. They came to Earth with the humans who fled their dying worlds far out in space. These humans settled in Atlantis and spread their knowledge of civilization among the humans already here. After the fall of Atlantis and the persecution of magical species, the dragons withdrew into another plane of existence. Gradually, the dragons made brief appearances to the people in this timeline.

As we became more open to the possibilities of life in the astral plane and other timelines, the dragons decided to become more open to passing on information.

The Star Born and the Star-Moon Clans were formed during the voluntary exile. The Star Born decided to include only specialized groups into their clan; the Star-Moon Clan is much more social, providing humans with co-magicians, teachers, and guardians.

The Star Born dragons have five claws. Sometimes members of both clans have three upper front fangs. Star Born members also interact the least with humans, and they are primary colors and shades, with indistinct spots, stripes, or patches. They wear the Great Seal of the Dragon pendant. They are definitely very aloof.

The Star-Moon Clan looks much the same as the Star Born dragons do. However, they work with humans and other beings all the time. They distinguish themselves from the Star Born by wearing a simple five-pointed star pendant. If they don't have feet with four claws, they have long, featherlike manes. They also have many related clans that make up the major clan.

She Who Sleeps has become She Who Naps. This ancient dragon of wisdom, who dwells near the gates to the Highest level of the Otherworld, suddenly awoke just before the influx of the new clans. Because of this influx of beleaguered clans, she now takes an active presence in this Earth plane again. She is one of the oldest dragons, along with Tiamat, Zee, Alt Mumit, and a few others. As a dragon ages, its hide becomes thicker and imbedded with magickal powers. This imbedded power can be felt from quite a distance away, even by humans.

The dragons of the elements were among the first dragons to appear again in this world, at least as I observed them. The first actual dragons that caught my attention were the two fledgling guardians who arrived unannounced. They opened my psychic eyes to a complete species that interacted with this world and humans on an almost daily basis. I was surprised to learn of all the other types of dragons who lived in the immediate astral realm surrounding us.

Star Born

The leaders of the Star Born Clans are Zarsa and her mate Suryon. There are two distinct groupings of dragon species that were here before the influx of migrating dragons. These are very specialized groups that cover a number of very important functions. All members of the Star Born group have five claws on their feet. The Star Born rarely have subclans. They also interact the least with humans.

Chaos

Most work full-time within the Void; a few of them work full-time with the Light and Dark Dragons of the Star-Moon Clan. Their leader is Ziri Kaar. Their colors are very dark, such as black, gray, magenta, purple, and green. They are the largest of the Star Born except for the Savage Heart Clan of warriors. Their chaos and destruction are primarily to create something better; old ideas, old forms, and old ways of living must be broken down and re-created. Everything is required to keep growing and changing, or it is recycled into another, more productive form. I was taught that the most effective magician is one who uses a balanced blend of light and darkness.

These dragons represent the negative power currents necessary to dissolve problems and sweep away troublesome people. They are of very dark colors: black, gray, pewter, iron, dark magenta, purple, reds, and greens so dark that they look nearly black. Their bodies are heavy and huge; in fact, they are the largest of all dragons. Their wide wedge-shaped heads sit atop long necks. Their serpentine tails are either barbed or have a spiked knob on the end. Enormous wings carry them on flights.

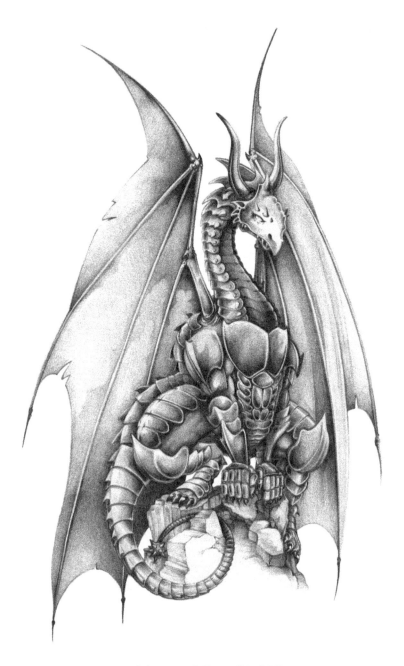

STAR BORN CLAN

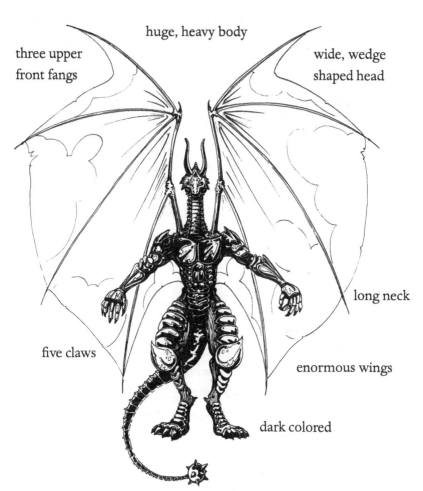

three upper front fangs

huge, heavy body

wide, wedge shaped head

long neck

five claws

enormous wings

dark colored

serpentine tails are barbed or have a spiked knob on the end

STAR BORN CLAN

When these dragons make changes and help in rituals, they do everything in a big way. They go past your limited view of happenings, straight to the heart of the problem, so be certain you can stand their help before you call on them. These dragons work with re-creation of lives, relationships, and careers; breaking of barriers; changing luck; vast changes in general; work on past lives; divination; the confining of enemies or anyone who will hinder your forward growth or movement.

Chaos dragons are connected with death and rebirth more than others of all dragons. When using them in an attempt to destroy barriers and remove enemies, one often finds oneself face to face with oneself, the worst enemy of all.

> *Transformation is my will.*
> *Use your power, my desire to fill.*
> *I thank you, dragons old and wise,*
> *Of Earth and Fire, Water, Skies,*
> *For sharing wisdom here with me.*
> *As I will, so shall it be.*

Cloud Masters

Also known as the Metal Masters. Their leader is Hahdatai. This dragon clan taught all blacksmiths on all worlds and all levels how to work with the metals on their planet. They are hues of the metallic substances with which they work.

Fire Heart

Historians for all the Star Born dragons, concerning their Multiversal work. Their leader is Mesh-lam. Aldram, Keeper of the Book, is from this clan. They also are responsible for keeping records on where, when, and how the dragons find the Annihilator, with the hope that a pattern will show that will allow the dragons to destroy this sentient evil. They are of the general Star Born colors, but have a pulsating red glow in their chests just behind their great Seal pendant.

Gem Masters

Also known as White Dragon Breath, this clan carefully watches the stones on all planets for changes. Such changes predict the health of the planets. The leader is Uurnos. These dragons have the chameleon-like quality of blending in with their surroundings.

Mystic Star

These are the spiritual teachers of the four Mystery Schools at the center of the Five Rings. They are also called the Hidden Dragons. Dragons and humans can only receive this higher learning if they pass the tests of the Five Rings. The head of Healing is Durka. He has the European dragon shape of a heavy, broad body. The triangular head sits at the end of a long sinuous neck. His snakelike tail ends in a barbed tip. His two leathery wings are long and strong. Ridges of thick, sharp-edged scales frame the eyes, which are golden with rims of greenish yellow. His claws are steel gray. Durka is covered with scales in colors of green, from pale green to almost black.

The head of Divination and Prophecy is Hun-Tun. Her scales are a kaleidoscope of shades of yellow-gold and orange. Although her body resembles a very thick, long snake, she has small front feet with black claws. Her scales change colors and patterns when she moves. The two small wings on her back by her back legs have diamond patterns. Her head is long and narrow and merges with her body, which has no neck. Her piercing eyes are a glittering black. Three red stripes run parallel to each other from the tip of her nose to the end of her pointed tail.

Im-Miris teaches advanced techniques of magick in the school at the third and Southern Gate. He reminds one of the dragons of Babylon and Chaldea, as he has a thick body and head with the blunt muzzle of a huge canine. His four paws have four dark red claws. His two front feet are shaped like lion paws, while the two back feet are reminiscent of huge bird feet. He has two wings with feather-like scales. His overall coloring is a mixture of rich desert hues, brick red, and deep sparkling brown. His scales resemble short, fine hair, but are actually hard and semi-shiny. His neck is short, like that of an animal, and his glittering eyes are bright red.

Gark-Yin teaches the very in-depth class of Advanced History in the school at the Western Gate. This history covers all the planets in the galaxy and all timelines. She is an azure blue Eastern dragon with gold edging on her scales. Red thread-thin whiskers wave from above her eyes and around her nose. Her long slender body has four legs with four dark gold claws on each foot. These legs are small in proportion to her body. Her antennae are colored in a beautiful pattern of gold, azure blue, and pure red, twisting and turning as she senses the air for changes in vibration, especially in the emotions and mental thoughts. She has no wings. Her golden-brown eyes are watchful but compassionate.

Rainbow

They balance the Multiversal energy flows that affect the dragon eggs and young ones in Dragon World. In other words, it is their duty to provide the best atmosphere so that their species might survive. They are led by Beh-Raph-Bo. Their brilliant coloring fluctuates according to the energy flows that brush against them.

Savage Heart

Warriors and Gate guardians to all Gates to areas of the Otherworld and throughout the Multiverse. Their leader is Arallu. Like the Fire Heart Clan, these are the usual Star Born hues. However, they have a distinct mark of two overlapping hearts on their foreheads. When calm, this mark wavers between blue and green. When they are working with other warriors and guarding Gates, this mark changes to colors between yellow and orange. When they attend a Dragon Warrior's initiation, the mark glows softly with all shades of lavender, purple, gold, and silver. When a Savage Heart is engaged in fighting negative energy, this mark flashes streams of blood-red light.

Snow

A subclan of the Rainbow Clan, they are messengers and creative helpers throughout the Multiverse. Their leader is Eeza. They are colored like brilliant golden sunlight overlaid with sparkling crystalline snow. The beautiful Snow dragons are special messengers. They have a mercurial temperament that matches the planet Mercury, or its equivalent, in every system of the Multiverse. They tend to withdraw slightly during our Mercury retrograde times.

Ordinarily, the Snow dragons are constantly busy carrying new ideas for inventions, the arts, and all types of activities throughout the Multiverse, seeding them on all planets everywhere. Also, they act as messengers from deities, guides, guardians, and angels to people.

Star-Moon

The leaders of the Star-Moon Clans are Etinera and her mate Steft.

The Star-Moon dragons all have four claws on their feet. If not, they have long, featherlike manes. This group has many subclans that make up a major clan. Also, they work with humans and other beings all the time. They distinguish themselves from the Star Born by wearing a simple five-pointed star pendant. The Star Born are definitely very aloof, while the Star-Moon are more into helping humans better themselves and our world.

Air dragons are led by Sairys (pronounced sair'iss) and are all in shades of yellow. Air dragons belong to a family whose related species include those of wind, storm, and weather. Sairys

STAR-MOON CLAN

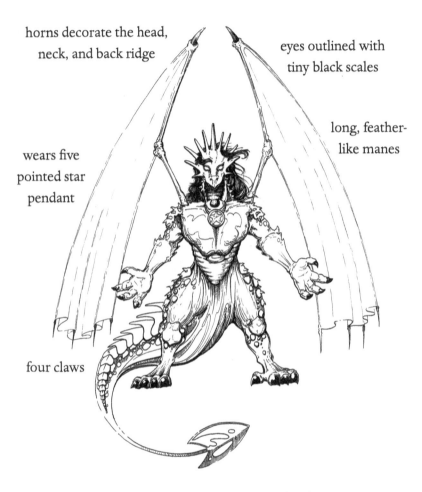

horns decorate the head, neck, and back ridge

eyes outlined with tiny black scales

long, feather-like manes

wears five pointed star pendant

four claws

tail shaped like an arrowhead

STAR-MOON CLAN

is sunflower-yellow on the back but a much lighter shade on the belly and wings. Tan stripes decorate her wings, being deepest in color over the wing bone skin. The tail is shaped like an arrowhead; an array of uneven, outward pointing horns decorate the head, neck, and back ridge. The eyes are outlined with tiny black scales.

> *Dragon ruler of wind and cloud,*
> *I call your secret name aloud.*
> *Sairys!*
> *Quicken my mind, renew my life.*
> *Grant me joy free from strife.*
> *Sairys!*

Dragons of the air element belong to a family whose subspecies include those of wind, storm, and weather. At times they join forces with those of fire, volcanoes, seas, mountains, forests, and chaos.

Fire dragons come in every shade of red, orange, and dark reddish-yellow. Led by Fafnir (faf'neer), these are related to the species of desert and arid regions, and sometimes work with those of chaos and destruction. They are connected with all kinds of fire, including volcanoes and lightning.

Fafnir is a rich scarlet red; the wing bone skin is a mottled red and yellow. There are uneven lengths of horns from the tip of the nose to the tip of the arrowhead tail. Its oval eyes have a yellow iris with a black slit.

> *In your cavernous, fire-filled hall,*
> *Echoes the name that I now call,*
> *Fafnir!*
> *Stir my blood with willpower bold.*
> *Create new changes from the old.*
> *Fafnir!*

Fafnir also oversees the sunbeams, noon, summer, any kind of helpfulness, the sun, blood, enthusiasm, activity, change, passion, courage, daring, willpower, and leadership. Negative associations are hate, jealousy, fear, anger, war, ego, conflicts, lightning, volcanoes, and harm for any kind.

Water dragons are led by Naelyon (nail'yon). Their duty is to oversee dragons of the seas, springs, lakes, ponds, and rivers. They are shades of blue. They help balance emotions with compassion, peace, and intuition. On the negative side, they work in floods, rainstorms, whirlpools, lack of emotional control, and any kind of harmful water.

Naelyon has a pale blue underbelly with mottled darker blue patches on its sides and back. Its four legs are shorter than most other dragons and are webbed between four of the toes, leaving the fifth as a thumb. It has a thin upright membrane down its back that is the same shade as the belly. Instead of hard horns, this dragon has multiple flexible antennae, which can stiffen if needed as weapons.

> *Calm water, moving water, seas and lake,*
> *I call upon the water drake,*
> *Naelyon.*
> *Teach me the psychic. Grant to me calm*
> *And peace of mind, compassion warm.*
> *Naelyon!*

Positive associations of water are sunset, autumn, any form of helpful water, compassion, peacefulness, forgiveness, love, intuition, calmness, and peace of mind. Negative associations are floods, rainstorms, whirlpools, any kind of harmful water, laziness, indifference, instability, lack of emotional control, and insecurity. It is not unusual to find this element working with dragons of wind, storm, weather, mountains, forest, or those of destruction.

The leader of the earth element is Grael (grail). These large dragons have mostly clear, dark green scales interspersed with shimmering scales like gemstones. Their duty is to oversee the mountains and land in general; also minerals, gems, caves, and the moon and moonbeams. These are the most placid of the species, although they stir up disruptive energies when they become angry, which causes massive earthquakes.

Grael's scales are a deep emerald green and automatically change shades so the dragon is camouflaged. It has a long neck, an iridescence to the edges of its scales and four feet. Its back has a row of sharp rounded horns that go completely down to its pointed tail.

> *From your mountain caverns deep,*
> *Rise, northern dragon, from your sleep.*
> *Grael!*
> *Lead me to riches, purpose true,*
> *Endurance, strong. I call on you.*
> *Grael!*

Positive associates of the earth element are midnight, winter, mountains, gems, caves, soil, respect, endurance, responsibility, stability, prosperity, thoroughness, and purpose in life. Negative associations are rigidity, unwillingness to change or see another side of a problem, stubbornness, lack of conscience, vacillation, earthquakes, and slides. The subspecies of this element are those of the mountains and forest, and those of the desert and arid regions (the latter shared with Fafnir).

Two dragon species are considered to command the center of the magickal circle; these balance all the elements, so none gains control over the others. Using this balance of energy helps the magician to bring more positive intent to manifestation. These dragons follow a higher guidance of the greatest kind, far beyond our ability to understand. Universal laws will not allow static conditions, or vastly over-balanced ones, to exist for any length of time. Everything is in motion; nothing stays still. These are the light and dark dragons.

The dragons of light handle positive currents of magickal energy. Their primary duties include the sun and daylight, any spiritual growth, the balancing of karma, and helping the magician to develop psychic guidance. They exist in a strange bubble where primordial matter is constantly being sent to blend with dark energy.

The leader of the light dragons is Llan Vys, a very pale lavender-gray with white belly scales. Other colors are ivory, orchid, and lilac. A thin membrane of glistening white runs down their back to the end of their pointed tail. Their round eyes are golden with a circular pupil. The light dragons (light of the spirit) rule positive power currents in magick. They are associated with all forms of day, the sun, reaching toward the spiritual, balancing karma, seeking the truth, bettering life on all levels, positive attitude toward all things, psychic guidance, and helpful light magick. Negative associations are self-righteousness and an "I have the only way" attitude.

Light of the spirit,
symbol of Sun,
Be with me now 'til this
spellworking's done.
Help me to balance all
karma and force
'Til I reach to the truth
of my life on this Earth.
Guide me and teach me,
O dragons of Light.
Sparkle my magick with
power on this Night.

The dragons of dark control negative currents of energy and weave this into the positive stream of energy handled by the dragons of light. Dark dragons are usually a shade of gray or light black. They rule over the moon and stars, psychic guidance, balancing karma, and seeking the truth. They too live in an isolated bubble of primordial matter, from which they send energy to blend with light.

The dark dragons are mostly a medium shade of matte black with a lighter-shaded membrane running down their back to their pointed tail, though the range is always in degrees of dark purple to almost black. Their eyes are also round, but with a black iris and a round white pupil. They are led by Nalm Kor. Sometimes they have silver sprinkles across their scales, like stars.

Dragons of Darkness, your power will run
Until the time of my magick is done.
Teach me your secrets, the dark not to fear,
For dark is receptive, not terror or tear.
Dreams of the Spirits, soar with the night.
Wrap me in guidance, you balance of Light.

The dark dragons (dark of the spirit) rule negative power currents. They are associated with all forms of night, the moon and stars, rest, dreams, psychic guidance, balancing karma, seeking the truth, and helpful dark magick. The negative associations are deep anger, hate, fear, unjustified revenge, working against karmic patterns, distorting psychic messages so that you hear what you want to hear, and harmful dark magick. They break down forms of energy to be re-created in a new form. They work with the light dragons in this manner.

The light and dark dragons rule the center of the circle and balance all the other elements. Through invocation of light and dark, the magician is able to mix a blend of elements that will bring forth the desired manifestation. This draconic family works with all the other elements, but particularly with those of chaos, when breaking down and remaking something.

The dragons of storm are elemental in a different way. They take the four elements called up by the magician and mold them with the magickal intent of the spellcasting. They also work with the weather during seasonal changes. They are easier to see, feel, and work with during storms and other more drastic weather-energy changes.

The storm dragons are a camouflage of black and stormy gray. Their scales often glisten as if wet. Their eyes are slanted with a rounded gray iris and black pupil. They have extra hands at the elbow bend of the wings.

> *The winds are howling through the trees.*
> *The clouds are racing 'cross the sky.*
> *The weather is changing once again.*
> *Great dragons are passing by*
> *By thought I follow your airy dance*
> *Through mountains of clouds above so High.*
> *Bring us good weather for this land.*
> *Great dragons, pass on by.*

Along with these main, and specifically trained, dragons are four more of even greater power and position. These are called the four hidden dragons of the four hidden gates at the center of the five inner rings. These dragons do not interact with humans unless a human has worked her/his way through the studies of the five inner rings.

As no one element works totally alone, elemental dragons join their great powers with other elementals to accomplish tasks.

Astra-Keepers

They work with the energies of the planets, days, zodiac, the nodes of the moon—in other words, astrology in general. There are dragons of these individual energy flows, but they have no major leader. They have midnight-blue wings, with this color spreading faintly onto their white body at the chest area. The subgroups working with the planets and such have individual and different coloring.

Storm-Bringers

This clan works with the elusive but powerful storm element. They also work with certain chaos dragons. Leader of Storm: Charoseia. Leader of Chaos group: Ziri Kaar. The Storm-Bringers are a smoky black with slashes of lightning white on their backs.

Time-Flight

These work with the elements and seasons, helping to blend energies into a repeating, logical year. They have leaders of individual groups, but no major leader. They appear in all true bright colors.

Web-Weavers

They work with seers of sacred geometry (the Quimisi), seers of all time, co-magicians, and ring initiators. Leader: Aia Cardya. There are also separate leaders for each smaller clan. This clan is a mixture of glittery and somber colors, marked with mystical symbols. The scales of some look like a mask around the eyes, a silver cap, or head ornaments hanging on the forehead.

Moon Quarters

1. Yen-lamar of the first quarter; very pale pearlescent blue.

2. Memezah of the full moon; iridescent white.

3. Unteekah of the third quarter; very pearlescent lavender.

4. Jyn-Kuaan of the new moon; iridescent black.

North Node of the Moon

Nadra Tho. As part of the Astra-Keepers, she is a silver-blue moonstone shade with a royal blue head. Her forehead is marked in black with the Ascending Node.

South Node of the Moon

Nadrica Thysa. Also part of the Astra-Keepers, her body is a multicolored shimmer in black moonstone with a royal blue head. Her forehead is marked in black with the Descending Node symbol.

Sun

Salaquet. Colors: yellow and gold.

Moon

Memezah. Colors: intermingling, changing pale colors of lavender, silver, blue, and pearl white.

Mercury

Talm. Colors: multiple shades of orange.

Mars

Durankayta. Color: red.

Jupiter

Yanizar. Colors: medium blue and purple.

Saturn

Bulla Kasz. Colors: black and indigo.

Uranus

Keetan. Color: iridescent blues and blue-greens.

Neptune

Vunoket. Color: sea-green.

Pluto

Zeiirahnak. Colors: deep reds and maroon.

Asteroid Belt

Fylufor: This dragon has been called Lucifer by some and belongs to the Astra-Keepers. Fylufor has the unique ability to change colors from sky blue with irregular spots of glowing white moonstone scale to sunrise pink with glowing pearlescent scales. However, his usual color of pewter gray always shows somewhere on his body. His actions sometimes appear to affect planetary events in an unpredictable manner. All his orders for activities come directly from the Great Goddess and the God, which is the same as saying from the Divine Source.

His influence covers not only the asteroid belt but much smaller globes, Ceres, and others.

Spring Equinox
Eiglis is yellow-green and works with the air element.

Summer Solstice
Suuriy glows a garnet red and works with the fire element.

Autumn Equinox
Shadalyn appears smoky brown and works with the water element.

Winter Solstice
Aettall is a very watery blue and works with the earth element.

Air Element
Sairys. Color: yellow.

Fire Element
Fafnir. Color: red.

Water Element
Naelyon. Color: blue.

Earth Element
Grael. Color: dark green.

Storm Element

Charoseia. Color: stormy gray.

Dragons of the mountains and forests are of the earth element. They generally have the look of Western dragons, with the heavier body, four legs, huge wings, long neck, and tail. Mountain dragons are much heavier-looking in the body than those of forests.

Dragons of the mountains and forests help to build long-lasting foundations in life: long-range goals, stability, physical and mental endurance, responsibility, and oftentimes the strength to stand up under existing responsibilities; they also give enduring prosperity and success that comes through personal effort and planning.

Forest dragons inhabit stretches of deep forests, groves, sometimes solitary clusters of trees. They like the changing patterns of sunlight through the branches and leaves. They tend to get upset and sometimes belligerent if their forests are damaged or destroyed without a good explanation.

Both mountain and forest dragons have been known to inhabit areas close to human towns and farms. Sometimes this creates a conflict, sometimes not, depending upon the behavior of the humans.

Some of the dragons are of the variety that at one time lived in or around barrows or burial mounds, especially if there was treasure inside.

Forest dragon, slithering, gliding,
Silent among the forest trees.
Ancient strength will you provide me.
Self-assurance, rest, and peace.

Dragons who dwell in the seas, lakes, rivers, ponds, and other bodies of water are basically shaped with small leg and wings; they are usually shaped like Asian dragons. They are a variety of shades of blue, from silver-blue to dark blue-green. All of them have a silvery, damp hue to their scales with some shade of blue predominant on the belly scales. They have feathery fringes about their mouths and down their backs. They have large horny eye sockets set in a rather flat snakelike head. They can be very large or rather small, depending upon their dwelling place. Dragons of the seas and various waters help with emotions, either calming them or breaking through a barrier built around them; movement, both to get events moving and to keep things fluid; calmness on all levels of being and in circumstances; and creating changes, especially those brought about by breaking free of people who control us through our emotions.

Dragons of the seas and waters, power,
I call upon you this magickal hour.
Raise my spellcasting to a new height.
Fill me with purpose, power, and light.

Power of Water, moving and bright,
Endless, eternal. Empower this night!

Wind, Storm, and Weather

Dragons of wind, storm, and weather in general belong to a subspecies of air dragons. They are long, slender dragons, some of them with great gauzy wings, others with the Eastern "flying lump" on their foreheads. Down the spine of the back flutters thin fringes of membrane tissue. They tend to be pale yellows and blues but can change to angry red-orange, purple, or black when calling up storms. Long feathery antennae rise above their eye ridges.

Dragons of this type are excellent helpers to control excesses in the weather; get things moving in your life, especially in the areas of creativity and the mental processes; and also for protection, flexibility of the mind, openness to new ideas, and sweeping away obstacles most often in a dramatic fashion. Sometimes these dragons have feather-looking scales that surround their eyes and necks.

These dragons inhabit cloud banks or very high mountain peaks where the winds never cease. Some Eastern weather dragons live in pools and ponds. They are in almost constant motion, riding the breezy air currents or roaring along with a whistling gale. Sometimes two or more of them join forces, either in play or a temporary dispute, thereby creating tornadoes and hurricanes. When they roll together, lightning and thunder occur.

WIND, STORM & WEATHER CLAN

long and slender

long, feathery antennae
above eye ridges

lizard-like

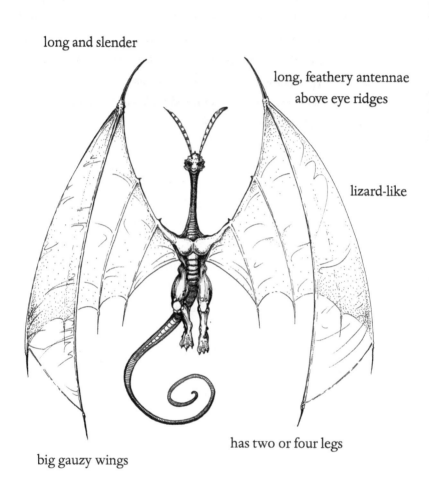

big gauzy wings

has two or four legs

WIND, STORM & WEATHER CLAN

The Australian Rainbow Serpent falls into the category of both weather and water dragons. It is known as a rainmaker in Australia, North America, and West Africa. From the deserts of Arizona to the peaks of the Andes, the great Feathered or Plumed Serpent Quetzacoatl was known as a kindly benefactor and rainmaker. He had multicolored scales and bright feathers about his neck and head.

> *The winds are howling through the trees.*
> *The clouds are racing 'cross the sky.*
> *The weather is changing once again.*
> *Great dragons are passing by.*
> *By thought, I follow your airy dance,*
> *Through mountains of clouds above so high.*
> *Bring us good weather for this land.*
> *Great Dragons, pass on by.*

Desert and Arid Regions

Dragons of the desert and arid regions can be of either elemental fire or earth, or both. These dragons help with prosperity, manifestations into the physical realm, and the removal of obstacles, especially in conjunction with air dragons. Dragons whose territories are dry and rather on the cool side tend to be earthy types, while those who reside in hot and dry climates are fire.

These dragons range in shades of brown, tan, white, and other colors that match their dry surroundings. However, they also have chameleon-like abilities to change colors, a perfect camouflage to avoid detection by humans.

They are serpentine in shape, with long slender tails, rather like those of lizards. The larger desert dragons often have huge, membranous wings, but there are subspecies of small desert dragons who have extremely small wings that are actually no good for flying. They use these stubs of wings to create whirlwinds of sand and dust.

They have either two or four legs which are very powerful, enabling them to move rapidly. They run quite fast over the desert and can easily outdistance a camel. A heavy ridge of bony socket overshadows the deep-set eyes, giving shade from the hot sun. They have a powerful hypnotic gaze that can cause their hunters and enemies to forget that they saw the dragon. Tightly overlapping scales keep out the sand and fine dust. These dragons are the most difficult for humans to communicate with, since they have been the target of hunters for centuries. They move around as well at night as during the day.

Desert dragons will build their lairs in rocky outcroppings or deep in areas of sand dunes. The sand-dwellers make a cave by mixing their corrosive saliva with sand, which hardens to produce super-tough walls that will weaken only under heavy incursions of water.

These dragons are very territorial, spending their lives in one area. Like all species, they have very long lives and exceptional mental abilities and thus know the locations of all ancient, long-lost cities and civilizations that are now covered by sand. Desert dragons can be unpredictable and difficult to work with.

> Desert heat and wind so cold,
> Aid me, I ask, O dragon bold.
> Nourish this seed of magick spell,
> That I might gain my spoken will.
> Bring life to this dream,
> Raise my magick power higher.
> Desert heat and wind so cold,
> Aid me, I ask, O dragon bold.

Fire and Volcanoes

Fire and volcano dragons are of the fire element and are in all shades of red, orange, and deep yellows. They have thick heavy bodies and long snakelike necks and tails. Some of them sleep in dormant volcanoes for long periods of time before they once again become active. These dragons are also visible in forest fires and large structure blazes. They are very unpredictable, unreliable, and difficult to work with. They will do as they please with a magician's spell. They will achieve the asked-for end result, but may "burn" their way through everything to get there.

These dragons help with personal purification on all levels of being: energy, courage, and stamina to pursue goals and finish projects and remove obstacles and barriers. They will go through and over anything and anyone to achieve the goal. The results can be swift and difficult to handle emotionally.

These dragons are capable of changing their size, appearing to grow as the fire or volcano gains in strength and power. It is possible to see very tiny fire dragons in your own fireplace or campfires. Ancient magicians called these "salamanders."

> *Crackle, burn, dragon turn*
> *night to day. Send good my way.*
> *Bring change within my range.*
> *Transform all at my call.*
> *Lift my thoughts higher, like your fire.*
> *Crackle, burn, dragon turn*
> *Night to day. Send good my way.*

The element of storm is controlled by the Storm-Bringers Clan, whose leader is Charoseia. Their color is a stormy gray. The energies of the element of storm lie between the traditional four elements and the void. Storm is an elusive but dynamic element that can block and redirect any elemental powers if a much more dramatic and lasting "balance" becomes necessary. Storm is a catalyst, a substance that creates great changes in other beings or events but isn't changed itself. Storm bursts into action when massive cleansing and rebalancing are needed, or when a speedy intellectual, mental, or spiritual awakening becomes vital. The recipient of this action may be a person, place, event, or even a galaxy.

The Star-Moon Clan includes the planetary, seasonal, and moon phase dragons. There are also two very unusual tiny dragon groups that are part of the Star-Moon Clan. The messengers of Tiamat are scarcely bigger than a large crow with a white ring of spikes across the top of the head. The wings are of tough membrane and resemble those of a bumblebee. The scales are a short hair-like type, and they have a short tail. The claws are more like bird feet with dragon talons and the tiny feet tuck up under their bellies. They were created by the great Tiamat simply to carry messages to humans in an unconventional manner. They also carry messages for Alt Mumit.

The Tam-Jin-Kee look exactly like dragonflies except for their pointed tails and feet. They are so easily mistaken for dragonflies that they stayed behind during the voluntary exodus. They call themselves "those who swarm and sting," although I've never known them to do this. They mimic the colors and flight patterns of dragonflies, so they are extremely difficult to spot.

Dragons are very fond of bright and shiny colors. They delight in pure shades in candle colors, and in gold, silver, copper, brass, bronze, and electrum in metals. They take absolute delight in the black shimmers within the void and deep space, as well as the rainbow flashes caused by bolts of positive energy and light. Their perception range with the color spectrum is deeper and far more accurate than ours.

The void is a place where no being can go except for the Chaos and Star Born dragons. The color black holds all colors within it, and the color of the void is black. It is the duty of the Chaos dragons to work in the void of unformed matter.

Dragon Ring Code

All throughout the Multiverse
The power is there to bless or curse.
'Tis balance of darkness and of light
That holds the Web threads ever tight.
Black Chaos dragons and those of Light,
Locked in balance that is right.
The dragons' code is very clear.
Each Ring should be for half a year,
From Apprentice to the Warrior guard,
The way to be Mystic is long and hard.
All levels explored, all truth laid bare,
The students' motives, pure as Air,
Must pass the test within the heart,
Before the Veil of Knowledge parts.
Dragon-trust he must earn, then wait
Until his teachers reveal the Gate.
Dragon magick, strong and old,
Requires the student to be bold.
Cast the numbers three times three,
For that is what the power will be.
No dragon spell is weak or small,
For dragon magick conquers all.

TEN

THE NEW
DRAGON CLANS

The new clans came through time and space to this astral time because of pandemics or annihilation by some kind of evil semi-humanoid. Some clans escaped with very few survivors. These are carefully courted by other small clans. Some of the offspring are hybrids, while others exhibit only the lost clan traits. These dragons carefully control the breeding to restore the original depleted populations and still keep within the dragon laws of population control.

The Waters Clans

The Waters Clans are self-explanatory; they prefer to stay in or around rivers, lakes, waterfalls, and oceans. From their physical evolution, it is evident that they lived on worlds consisting of large bodies of water or that were mostly water. They still lay

WATER CLAN

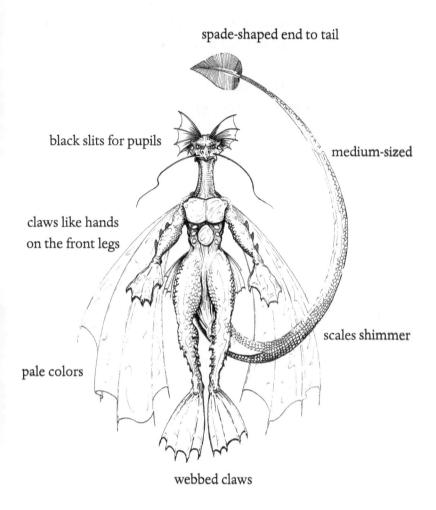

spade-shaped end to tail

black slits for pupils

medium-sized

claws like hands
on the front legs

pale colors

scales shimmer

webbed claws

WATER CLAN

their eggs and hatch their young on land. However, this is now done close to water in their own realm. In their old habitats, they were harpooned and shot for their leather-scaled hides and meat. The young hatchlings were clubbed to death for their soft, supple hides. The teeth and fangs were made into expensive, exotic jewelry. Only about sixty of the six clans managed to escape.

The Auroras

These are one of the medium-sized dragons. Their scales are fish-like and shimmer, changing from a brilliant reflection to a matte-looking finish depending on the way they move. Basically, they are white in color with subtle flashes of icy pale blue, faint pinks, and pale lavenders. They prefer to stay in the colder zones, such as the Arctic, Iceland, and such places. They have claws like hands on the front legs. Short spikes decorate the outside of the front and rear legs. They have a spade-shaped end to the tail. Their pale blue eyes have black slits for pupils. They do a dance-like flight in the Northern Lights.

Galaxy Waters

They have webbed claws except for the thumb-claw. Their wings are shorter than other dragons', and they are smaller in body also. Their tail resembles a whale tail. They prefer more remote areas. Their scales are overlapping and round, and are sometimes covered in spots of moss and algae from sunning on the moist rocks. Their golden eyes have cat-like slits. Their scales change from brilliant silver or gold to light gray, depending on the temperature and surroundings.

Raging Waters

These are sea-water colored, capable of shifting to suit the surroundings. They have a long, twisted horn on their nose, like a narwhal. This horn is very sensitive to weather and in guiding them where they want to go. Their small wings are more for moving than flying, although they do leap and semi-fly for short periods of time. They have one large dorsal fin like a shark directly behind their head; the other spikes down their back are much smaller. Their claws are webbed except for the thumb claw. Their tail ends in two wide fins. The pale gray eyes have blue slits. Although they are a small clan that lays their eggs near ocean water on remote island, they swim in all the major oceans except for the far north or far south.

Sea Foam

Their scales are bluish-green points that are larger near the head and smaller near the tail. They have a third set of claws that are "hands" on the elbow of their stubby wings. Their ears are only open holes. Their eyes are dark blue with black slits. They are not friendly to humans, especially fishermen, whose nets they destroy.

Silver Pearls

These dragons live in the Arabian Gulf, China Sea, and around India. Their coloring reminds one of an oyster shell, but the scales are short and rough with hair that runs from the neck to the tip of their short, pointed tail. Their head is a pearly white. Groups of sensitive antennae sprout around their head. Their six-clawed toes are covered in the same shagged hair-scales. They are shy creatures who lay their eggs on beaches in an alternate timeline. Their pale green eyes have dark green slits. They also have antennae on their chin that looks like a beard.

Sirrush

This strange clan is the mentally slow member of all dragons. They live in marshy land. They were called Lau by the Africans and Sirrush by the Babylonians. They prefer to hide under water; they have a foul odor and a honking call. The strong hind legs have claws with talons like a raptor. They use their shorter forelegs as well as lashing tails to rend anyone who annoys them. The long neck supports a serpent-like head, frilled like a lizard's but with a horn on the tip of the nose. Their scales are a very small, fine, flat gray.

The Wanderers Clans

The Wanderers Clans are so named because they are still searching for others of their clans. They still have hope they will find others, but so far this hasn't happened. These clans are the most friendly to humans, but are still distrustful. On their previous worlds they suffered deliberate genocide from humanoids because of overpopulation and hunting for sport. The hatchlings were considered as prestigious pets until they grew too large, and then they were destroyed. Out of thirteen clans, only one hundred eighty-two of the combined clans made it safely here. The Quimisi were the last of these to come through and are fewest in number.

WANDERERS CLAN

more bird-like look

slits in eyes are wider
at the center to give it a
diamond-shaped look

horns above eyes
curve forward

forked
tongue

dorsal fins are tiangluar
and irregular in shape

scales are long and
look like feathers

fan like tail

WANDERERS CLAN

Diamond Eyes

Another name for this clan is Weather Eyes. Their eyes can change color according to the weather wherever they are. They can also change weather. They migrate with the birds both in winter and summer. The slits in their dark golden eyes open wider at the center, giving a diamond-shaped look. The eye color changes from gold to stormy gray, depending upon their mood and/or the weather around them. Their scales are shades of gray and spotted with white. Their facial horns above their eyes curve forward. The dorsal fins are triangular, irregular in shape, and very sharp.

Dream Watchers

Some of this clan are shape-shifters; their names are Callia, Mujaji, Syrah, Noemi, and Yoshi. The latter is one of the younger, smaller dragons. Their scales are longer and narrower than usual and look like feathers. These feather-looking scales outline the front edge of the wings, then turn into the common bat-like membrane. The coloring is a bluish-gray, with light gray eyes. Their fan-like tail looks smooth when closed but flares when they get upset. Their feathered ears have three short spikes behind each one.

The Dream Watchers monitor for predictive dreams. When many dreamers have similar dreams of disasters, they notify the High Council where the decision is made whether or not they can prevent the disaster.

Golden Talons

This clan is headed by na-Chandrus and Esbosheth. Their coloring is red with an odd fringe of fine gold spikes around their face. They prefer the dry areas of Africa along the Red Sea and Ethiopia.

Their wing bones are colored a deep rich brown and have a third set of claw-hands on the forward bending wing elbow. The triangular overlapping scales are finely edged in copper coloring that matches their slitted eyes. The spiked back is also a deep brown with thin stripes running down to the belly. They spend their time in the desert and rocky outcroppings.

Inbetween Dwellers

These are rarely seen but are a major moving force within the universe. They open portals to other levels for clans to get through. They are alert on all levels and timelines. They sometimes briefly appear as lighted orbs. Their leader is Shwanaji.

It is unusual to get a glimpse of these elusive long, slender creatures with their knobby horns, short legs, and waving membrane down their backs to their pointed tail. Chameleon-like, they blend into their surroundings.

Napata

This clan has flexible petal-shapes surrounding their faces. When angry, these petals snap straight back into sharp folded points. Their pastel colors darken when upset. Their claws have almost humanlike thumbs. On the end of a catlike tail is what looks like a powder puff but is really a weapon that can stiffen into needle knives. They are / were diplomats but don't hesitate a second to take action if diplomacy is useless. No lie or half lie can get by them. They have had no previous contact with humanoids. Two hundred twenty-six came through the gates with no losses or injuries. They are of both earth and air qualities: practicality and inspiration. They are related to She Who Naps.

Orion Guardians

This was the first clan to come through on April 30, 2010. They came through without a fight, but only because of careful planning. Their scales resemble chain mail. They are shades of green, even their eyes. Looking at a group is like looking at a grove of mixed green trees. Some have smooth instead of rough scales.

They are very interested in unusual quartz crystals, as are the Quimisi.

Sage Crystals

The leaders of this clan are Bozjik and Niniiak. These dragons are silver-blue with long pointed horns on their foreheads. The long black tongue is forked. There are long, straight spikes on the back, rising in a random pattern of lengths. The yellow eyes are slanted in their narrow skulls. "Sage" in this context refers to wise elders. They work with the Quimisi and others on gathering knowledge.

Sand Dwellers

The leader is Sutekh, Lord of the Horses. His mate is Shil-Al-Ananika, which means Beautiful One. The clan is also called the

Kemeri Talons, which connects it in some way to Egypt. They have extra-large bronze-colored eyes with a horned shield down the nose. Their long, slender, tan body and stubby reddish-brown wings move them quickly under the sand of the desert Egyptian areas where they settled. The nictitating eye membrane keeps the sand out of their eyes. They build under the sand cave, hardened with their saliva. They know where all the ancient temples and cities are buried under the sand.

Scarlet Eclipse

Khirsrit and Syena are the leaders of this clan, which lives in the Sinai and ancient Persia, or what is now modern-day Syria, Iraq, and Iran. They are slightly different from the Sand Dwellers but often intermingle with them. This clan prefers the rugged cliffs, rocks, and caves of ancient Babylon and Ishtar's Gate. Their smooth, fine, tan scales are perfect for keeping out the sand, which they like to bathe in, using their stubby wings to whip up small dust clouds.

Sirus Wanderers

There are not many members of this clan. They often search planets in the Sirius galaxy for more survivors. They are heavy-bodied with large wings and a long spade-shaped tail. Like the Star Born, their colors go across the basic color spectrum. Their gold-bronze eyes have dark blue slits. They have spikes from the tip of their nose to the end of the tail. Their claw-hands have five fingers besides the thumb-claw. They also have a type of camouflage spattering of shades of their belly color across the body.

Star Singers

This clan is all shades of red and a little smaller in size than usual. They destroy by sound. These aloof creatures can cause cellular disruption by their singing. However, they will do this only in self-defense. Their scales are irregular in pattern, and they have four claw-fingers and a thumb. Their wings are narrow and sleek, with an arrowhead tail.

Triple Talons

Also called the Aziaks, this heavy-bodied dragon's scales are a camouflage mixture of browns and tans. The face is wide and long; the tail is a ball of spikes. The wings have short spikes along the front edges. The five finger-toes have two talons each that operate independently like pincers. The thumb-claw has only one talon.

The Quimisi

This was the last clan to come here. Alt Mumit (Wisest of All Grandmothers), an equal of Tiamat, came with them. They hold the repository of all ancient universal and dragon history, especially the spiritual history on all inhabited planets. They are very interested in unusual quartz crystals.

This clan is very few in number; because of their placidity, they lost most of their clan getting through the rift Veil. They fled their galaxy homes only at the last minute. Their scales look like a grid pattern. The color is a deep dark purple that only reflects the coloring when the light catches their movement. They have a ridge of nine twisted horns across the side and top of their heads. Some horns twist counterclockwise, while other twist clockwise. Their black feet have seven claw-fingers and a thumb-claw. There is a ring of small silver scales around their eyes, which are a rich goldish-bronze with black slits.

They also seem to be the holders of knowledge about many esoteric facts and sacred geometry, especially the strange Merkaba crystal. The Merkaba is a three-dimensional form of interlocking triangles. It is very possible that its name, shape, and uses came to this planet with the first immigration of the Atlanteans, then spread to Egypt before the islands sank.

The name *Merkaba* comes from the highest of ancient Egyptian Mystery Schools and is found in many languages, including Egyptian, Hebrew, and Zulu. In ancient Egyptian, *Mer* is a place of ascending, *ka* means the individual spirit, and *ba* is the "light vehicle," or astral body. It obviously refers to a time-dimensional movement, not death or dying. It controls time-shifting and the interaction of light dimensions. It can open the conscious mind to other dimensions of the Multiverse. It also amplifies the power of thought-forms and concentrated intent. If held during a meditation, the Merkaba helps with time travel and enhances the part of you that astral travels.

Dark Warriors Clans

The Dark Warriors were so fierce and consistent in their homeland disputes with humanoids that they were deliberately targeted by mutated viruses directly programmed at them. They were also attacked by huge armies of small, bright-red-colored humanoids. Those dragons infected by the viruses chose to

DARK WARRIORS CLAN

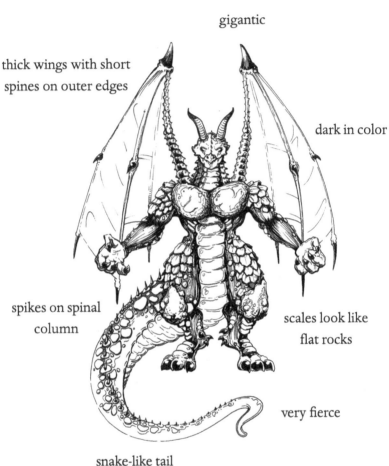

gigantic

thick wings with short
spines on outer edges

dark in color

spikes on spinal
column

scales look like
flat rocks

very fierce

snake-like tail

DARK WARRIORS CLAN

deliberately stay behind rather than risk spreading the disease. Clan numbers arriving here were small. At least one clan came through with only six members plus the remaining female of the leading pair. Dark Warriors are very aloof, suspicious of all humans, unpredictable, and least likely to be helpful.

Death Flyers

Gigantic and black, they have vertical pupils in gold eyes. Its tail has long, bronze colored spikes protruding every few inches down the spinal column. They lay granite-gray eggs. They are very unpredictable and can shoot fire well over one hundred feet. They are also called the Boshtark. Their leader is Yoshabel, the surviving female mate of their other dead leader.

Fate Furies

The main color is a dark slate splattered with black freckles. The slanted eyes in the wide head are a lighter slate color with black slits. The scales look like flat rocks. The tail has snake-like rattles and a stinger. The ears are long and webbed with folds. The rear legs are longer than usual with heavy muscles. The wings are thick and have short spines on the outer edges.

The Feathered Ones

This clan is a deep, dark green with an iridescent edge to its featherlike scales. It has a long slender neck with a narrow head. Its feet all have overhanging feather-scales. The same type of scales run down its neck and body. These scales are sharp and can stiffen upward when angry.

Judge Warriors

Also called the Cuzztah. Tutakushu and Zatasha are the leaders. This clan seems to be judges for any Dark Warrior disputes. Their midnight-blue scales are in irregular patterns with black spikes down their back and on both sides to the ball of their spiked tail. Their face and pointed ears have short fur-like coverings, long curved antennae, and a fur "mustache" that covers the nose.

Sessanans

Sessanan fire is blue in color. They are experts in battle tactics. Their leader is Serif. They have large, thick plating from the head to the tail as well as on the top of the legs and feet. They have two curved horns at the back of the head, and a row of forward-hooking triangles down the back. Feather-like scales protrude from the rear leg joints.

Shadow Seekers

This clan's dark matte-gray scales look like chain mail. Two pairs of wings have membrane webbing only halfway up the long, feathered bone struts. The belly is covered with overlapping plaques of thick scales while the back and tail are armored with a central row of spikes, plus two more rows on each side. The ear holes are partially covered by large fans of feathered scales.

Storm Stalkers

This clan also has weather-type eyes. The leader is Chaosia. The eyes are a dark blue with black slits but can change color according to the surrounding weather. It is the smallest of the Dark Warriors, with a long, slender, black body sprinkled with fiery red spots. Like some Asian dragons, it has no wings but instead a "flying horn" in the center of its forehead. Its hair-like mane and tail can stiffen into a myriad of needle knives when upset. Its four legs and feet are very small.

Thunder Wings

Also known as the Thunder Birds. Its irregular, overlapping scales are a mixture of sizes on the head, neck, upper body, and legs. Its stormy-gray color shifts like smoke across its thick body. The spikes down its spine are sawtoothed in shape; one huge spike is at the top bend of each wing. Its feet have three claw-fingers and a thumb-claw. It has wide heavy scales covering its chest and belly. Its yellow eyes have black slit pupils.

Time Riders

This clan goes forward and backward through time in various galaxies, gathering information. They share this with the Quimisi. Of medium size, the scales are a dark earth-brown with slightly lighter stripes curving from sharp spinal spikes down across the belly. The scales wrap completely around the tail, exposing just the sharp barb at the end. There are multiple straight and curved horns around the face and on the shoulders. The greenish-black slanted eyes have slit black pupils. The red tongue is long and forked.

War Magick

This clan is mostly invisible; they are also called the Kunjavi. They are highly skilled in the use of magick to defeat opponents. The scales are black with zigzags of dark gray irregularly running down to the belly. The eyes are yellow with black slits. Several pairs of antennae ring the narrow muzzle. The ears are short and pointed. A row of short triangular scales runs from the tip of the nose to mid-tail. The end of the tail is completely covered with spikes.

CONCLUSION

THE GREAT JOURNEY
CONTINUES

You will learn that some clans are simply too alien in their thinking or their dislike of humans to trust working with most magicians. However, these same clans may work well with some magicians. The last clans who were forced to cross from other timelines or levels are the least friendly or trustworthy. Because of past experiences, or simply because they haven't been around humans very long, they are highly cautious and aloof. One of each clan, however, seems to be reconnoitering and gathering information about humans; studying us intently until they come to a decision.

In turn, we need to remain as respectful of the more aloof and wary clans as we are of the rest of the dragon society. They are refugees of a sort, and we should respect that.

I know the new information I've included in this book is incomplete. However, perhaps all the great clans will be more agreeable and forthcoming in the future.

Your life is a path, a journey. Knowingly or unknowingly, you have been on a spiritual quest. It is good to have a dream, a vision, a positive plan for your future. From time to time, that pathway may be changed, as one is given new choices or faces unforeseen obstacles. It is difficult for us to see the final outcomes of these choices and changes. However, if you hold firm to your beliefs and continue to do the best you can at any moment, the path will again straighten out, and you will move forward. Be patient and persistent. The dragons will be beside you whenever you need help in making choices.

APPENDIX

The idea behind using planetary days and hours is that you are connecting with a stronger energy for use in your ritual. As the elements are the substance of the universe, the planets are more concerned with action and process. The ancients only used seven astrological planets: the sun, moon, Mercury, Venus, Mars, Jupiter, and Saturn. These planets also correspond to the days of the week and the hours of each day. To use this system, find the planet that corresponds to the type of ritual you plan to do. Next, select the proper day and hour in which to do it. Remember to adjust for daylight saving time if necessary.

Although the astrological nodes, asteroids, and outer planets are not often used in magickal practices, they are of real value to the magician who is willing to take the time to learn about them and their influences. The nodes of the moon, the five main asteroids, and planets beyond Saturn are not listed in the planetary hour charts. However, each of these bodies are considered to be higher aspect of other planets. You can therefore use the similar planet's hours to work with them.

The nodes of the moon, of course, are not actual physical bodies, but calculated points that relate the moon's orbit to the actual orbit of the earth around the sun. The ancient astrologers knew the nodes as knots or complications that they used in charting the heavens. They knew the north node as *Caput Draconis*, "head of the dragon," and the south node as *Cauda Draconis*, "tail of the dragon." When reading a natal chart, the lunar north node symbolizes the manner in which the individual takes in energy, events, and influxes, and any present life uses the person makes of that energy. The lunar south node points to the release of negative energies, memories, and/or habits. It also hints at past lives that still have an influence over the present life.

The new and waxing moon are the times for spells of increase, building, and growth; the full and waning moon are for taking apart or destroying things. Some things need to be taken apart or destroyed so that they can be made into something better.

Each planet has a dragon ritual chant for the physical, mental/emotional, and spiritual aspects of growth. These chants are to be used in conjunction with candles of the appropriate color.

You also can increase the energy by choosing to rub the candle with a corresponding oil and then rolling it in the appropriate crushed herbs. If you wish to carve any symbols or words into the candle, do so before oiling it. When oiling, do so from the wick to the bottom to bring things to you, and from the bottom to the wick to remove things. Leave the candle to burn out in a safe place. You also may insert the candle rituals into more formal ritual if you so desire.

It is proper etiquette to ask the dragons to join you in any dragon magick you do. Why should they join you if they aren't invited? And don't forget: you especially want your guardian and co-magician dragons with you!

To begin, hold the unoiled candle in your hands and chant the Charm of Making;

> *By glow of sun the power's begun.*
> *By moonbeam's light the spell is right,*
> *To create desire by Earth and Fire,*
> *Water, Air, make magick fair.*
> *Powerful Charm of Making,*
> *creative Magick undertaking.*
> *By storm, be formed!*

Dragons of the Planets

Sun

Day: Sunday

Rules: Leo

Rituals: health, healing, confidence, hope, prosperity, vitality, personal fulfillment, immediate family, life-energy, money, favor, honor, promotion, success, support of those in power, friendships

Physical Chant:

> *Strength of body, vitality,*
> *I ask that these you give to me.*
> *Sun dragon, look on me with favor*
> *That power, riches I may savor.*

Mental-Emotional Chant:

> *I need a boosts of confidence,*
> *A circle firm of friendships true,*
> *New hope that's based on truthfulness.*
> *Sun Dragon, for these I do thank you.*

Spiritual Chant:

> *I seed your gift of personal fulfillment,*
> *Harken, Sun Dragon!*
> *Grant me success on my spiritual path.*
> *Help me, Sun Dragon.*

Moon

Day: Monday

Rules: Cancer

Rituals: travel, visions, divination, dreams, magick, love, agriculture, domestic life, medicine, luck, feminine aspects, water, birth, time theft, emotions

Physical Chant:

> *I seek magick, deep and old,*
> *All the love my heart can hold,*
> *Green magick of the plants and Earth,*
> *Psychic gifts to aid rebirth.*

Mental-Emotional Chant:

> *Emotions and time are so hard to control,*
> *And to fathom, O power of the moon.*
> *Teach me your magickal rituals and ways*
> *That I may learn control, very soon.*

Spiritual Chant:

> *Views of the future that come in the night*
> *When the silver moon rides high in the sky,*
> *I seek instruction to unlock my Dreams*
> *That my spirit may grow and thrive.*

Mercury

Day: Wednesday

Rules: Gemini, Virgo

Rituals: intellect, memory, science, creativity, business, magickal spells, divination, prediction, eloquence, gift of tongues, speed, speech, writing, poetry, inspiration, improvement of mind power, healing of nervous disorders

Physical Chant:

> *Magick, the arts, success in my trade,*
> *Business wisdom and divination,*
> *These gifts I would gain for*
> *My physical growth*
> *And to help in my conjurations.*

Mental-Emotional Chant:

> *The steady fire of intellect*
> *The light of creativity,*
> *Inspiration and eloquence,*
> *I ask now that you send to me.*

Spiritual Chant:

> *The power of prediction*
> *to aid my fellow Man,*
> *Grant this, dragon of Mercury.*

Healing power for the mind and soul,
Teach me the uses, O dragon great!

Venus

Day: Friday

Rules: Taurus, Libra

Ritual: love, marriage, friendship, pleasure, beauty, artistic creativity, imagination, fertility, partnerships, sex, spiritual harmony, compassion, children

Physical Chant:

My heart and soul long
for true love and Friendships,
Dragon of Venus, share these gifts.
For through experiencing them,
I shall Become stronger.
Teach me the joys of true partnerships.

Mental-Emotional Chant:

Beauty comes in all disguises,
Even in creativity.
Imagination brightens the life.
Grants me mental fertility.

Spiritual Chant:

> *Harmony of the soul*
> *is a treasured gift.*
> *O Dragon of Venus, teach*
> *me spiritual Harmony.*
> *Compassion for all*
> *beings in all places*
> *I send forth on your*
> *great wings.*

Mars

Day: Tuesday

Rules: Aries, Scorpio

Rituals: energy, courage, battle, conflict, death, masculine aspects, surgery, physical strength, opposition, defense, endurance

Physical Chant:

> *Courage-fire, burn much higher,*
> *Energy, come, make me free*
> *Of others' will. Teach me still*
> *To be myself, above all else.*

Mental-Emotional Chant:

> *I prepare for battle against my enemies.*
> *Stand beside me, red Dragon.*

Our defense and endurance cannot be
Overthrown.
Together we shall be victorious.

Spiritual Chant:

Sometimes the conflict within my own soul
Keeps me from reaching my spiritual goal.
Lift the veil, and let me see
That often the negative is me.

Jupiter

Day: Thursday

Rules: Sagittarius, Pisces

Rituals: honor, riches, health, friendships, the heart's desires, luck, accomplishment, religion, trade and employment, treasure, legal matters

Physical Chant:

Grant me honor and success.
Change my luck and make me bold.
Give me riches and happiness.
All you give my life can hold.

Mental-Emotional Chant:

> *Goals in life are needed*
> *To bring peace to the mind.*
> *Goals for Hand and intellect,*
> *Send, O dragon kind.*

Spiritual Chant:

> *Any task I can accomplish*
> *With your aid, Jupiter dragon.*
> *Spiritual paths open before me,*
> *Set my feet on the right path.*

Saturn

Day: Saturday

Rules: Capricorn, Aquarius

Rituals: knowledge, familiars, death, reincarnation, protecting buildings, binding, overcoming curses, protection in general, retribution, duties, responsibilities, influences, doctrines

Physical Chant:

> *Clear out the negative. Bring in the good.*
> *Bind up my enemies, curses, and all.*
> *Protection for me and my loved ones here*
> *Send from your great dark hall.*

Mental-Emotional Chant:

> *Responsibilities and duties*
> *should not Weigh down*
> *The body and mind as mine have done.*
> *Show me the karma that I must smooth*
> *So the battle might be won.*

Spiritual Chant:

> *Through the coils of mists and time*
> *I seek my karmic paths to know.*
> *That I might reach new heights sublime*
> *And spiritually expand and grow.*

Dragon Speak

Since dragons prefer to use telepathy rather than verbal communication with humans, I asked them for a few dragon words for humans speaking to other humans. Following is a list with the dragon words phonetically written out. If two letter As are written, both are sounded out.

Greetings everyone	En yal
Well met (to dragons)	Onkkyla
Well met (to humans)	On mila
Farewell	Zar yalto

Rest well	Synta natal
Until next we meet	Onkyla a'a shunan
Did I do well?	A'yee sylvim?
Yes	Bytah
No	Negta
Are you finished?	Net rwi a'ah kyp?
Do you understand me?	Net doraratia?
What is your name?	Kylan a net?
Where is the meeting?	Contoo a'a cirklo?
Help me!	Taloo kee yee!
Look!	Baynto!
Be careful!	Mish cortush!
I'm sorry	Yee a rosa
I agree with you	Yee a compleex
I wish to speak!	Yee seejah!
Ancient Ones	Hyl Agisho
My friend	Yea a'a dinsh

Dragon Respect Names

You should never call any dragon by its names unless you have been given direct permission to do so. To do otherwise is considered very rude, as is calling a dragon by just its clan name.

The following is a list of respect names, which will keep you out of possible trouble when meeting and communicating with any dragon:

Chasah: name for a leader of any clan. Meaning "leader" or "guide," this respect name is used whether the dragon is female or male. It is quite common for females to lead clans.

Mon-Tah: your teacher/co-magician, unless given permission to use their name.

Moon Gutash: Star-Moon clan members, except their young

Moosha: name for all gate guardians, who are members of the Savage Heart clan. The name means "warrior."

Mot-Tah: other teachers and co-magicians.

Star-Gutash: Star Born clan members, except young, who you are not ever likely to see.

Tad-Ekam: name for any Chaos dragon.

Tah-Soor-Izoris: the Elders and very important dragons you meet.

Tika: a general child-name for the small and guardian dragons of any clan.

Sacred Geometry

Sacred geometry, also known as the Platonic solids, have been considered some of the most spiritual symbols in the Mediterranean area since the time of the philosopher Plato. Still today in Judaism, these figures are studied as a holy path to the highest spiritual paths. Others study them as a high branch of numerology. Rather than confuse the reader over the many spiritual explanations, I am using the design of sacred geometry as symbols to further the power of magickal spells.

The Quimisi have the greatest knowledge of sacred geometry, along with the star symbol magic. As they were the last clan to come to this plane because of persecution, there is still much to be learned about and from them.

Circle: wholeness, potential ever-expanding cycles.

Triangle: beginning, middle, end; body, mind, spirit. It represents spirit, divinity, life, strength, harmony and completion. Upward facing, it is considered to be a symbol of fire and masculine energy. Downward facing, it is feminine energy, family, and water.

Tetrahedron: one of the five three-dimensional geometric shapes called Platonic solids. It has four equal triangular faces. Also called the Eye of the Dragon, it stands for fire, action, and understanding.

Square: an earthly substance, matter, security. The four directions. We honor our ever-expanding potentials by invoking the four directions inside a cast circle.

Hexahedron: a cube. Being a three-dimensional shape, it is one of the Platonic solids. It represents solidity, strength, confined order, substance, and stability.

Spiral: cosmic connection. The beginning, the germination, the seed from which all life springs. Human DNA is shaped as a double helix (a double spiral) that gives us a hidden store of knowledge and wisdom, called the fore or hidden light. Spirals express themselves in nature as wind, tide, and storm; internally as emotional upheaval and calm.

Pentagon: power and excellence. This five-sided geometric shape holds energy representing power, excellence, regeneration, and transcendence. When the midpoints of each side are connected, they form a five-pointed star or a pentagram, a symbol of power and protection. It represents your personal potential and the ability to transcend obstacles.

Hexagon: a six-sided geometric shape. It stands for structure, function, and order. Spiritually speaking, it is space, power, and time transmuted by consciousness. The energy's forms are fire and lightning, nuclear, and solar—all are active and dynamic but have the power to transmute something to something new.

Star Tetrahedron: A three-dimensional shape. It joins an upward-facing tetrahedron, representing masculine energy and fire, with a downward-faction tetrahedron, representing feminine energy and water. Interlocked together, they mean dynamic balance and expanded awareness. The shape is contained in the energy field surrounding your body. When activated, it forms a time-space vehicle of ascension called a *merkaba*. The *mer* (light), *ka* (spirit), and *ba* (body) union is a sacred one that responds directly to emotion. It stretches far beyond your everyday life and gets in touch with your Higher Self and universal wisdom. It represents a seeker of intuitive knowledge. It is an instrument of expanded awareness, multi-dimensional travel, the path toward ascension, co-creation, and togetherness.

Heptagon: a seven-sided polygon. It represents movement through cycles. Each action you take creates harmony or discord. Seven is a very sacred number in many cultures throughout history, and many things can be found grouped in series of seven: rainbow rays, musical notes, stages of transformation, and so on.

Octahedron: a shape with eight triangular faces, it is one of the three-dimensional Platonic solids. It helps to connect to your inner child. Honor the inner messages you receive. It embodies sympathetic magick, phases of the moon, and periodic renewal. Eight multiplied by eight equals sixty-four. There are sixty-four known codons in human DNA. The figure eight lying on its side is the symbol of infinity. Nourishment and the air element.

Infinity Symbol: represents the balance of all expressions of consciousness. It is an unbroken wholeness in flowing movement. Act from the place of hope and clarity of intention.

Nonagon: coming from the greatest single-digit number, it is a boundary. It is a trinity of trinities, three times three. It represents perfection, balance, and order. It is the ultimate extension, achievement, and completion. The completion of a cycle in your life. You have given your all and contributed your best. Now you stand at the gateway of something entirely new.

Dodecahedron: one of five three-dimensional figures called Platonic solids. This shape holds cosmic wisdom within its structure. This geometric has twelve equal five-sides. It embodies divine thought or will. It stands for heaven, ether, prana, and feminine energy. This connects you with divine thought and with a realization of the universality of oneness. Moves away from the concept of duality into an experience of the oneness with your being. Universal love, unity, consciousness.

Icosahedron: a shape comprised of twenty equilateral triangular faces; one of the five three-dimensional Platonic solids. This shape will fit into a sphere. It represents the beginning of new consciousness as well as water, liquids, and feminine energy. Ask for inner guidance and allow the flow to enter your thoughts in a way that will release old patterns and bring light and higher wisdom. You will be surprised how easily you untangle the situation once you see it from a fresh vantage point. Seek a new perspective.

Star Pattern Magick

There is a long history in magick of using different shapes of stars to symbolize esoteric wisdom and Multiversal energies. The Quimisi Clan is quite adept at this knowledge. They study astronomy and astrology, and the heavenly galaxies in general. They use star symbols as magick, as protection, prevention, and to change things as they are led through the knowledge of their secret star magick. You can carve these symbols into candles or draw them out on paper to channel the energy you need into a spell.

The three-pointed star—a triangle—represents the balance of the three main levels of the Otherworld. Three is a mystical number that can give luck, courage, and endurance. The set of interlocking triple rings represents body, mind, and spirit.

There is one very special three-pointed star called the Eye of the Dragon. This is an ancient design much favored by gem cutters in medieval times. Traditionally, this cut was said to be very magickal and sacred to the nine muses. A four-pointed star cut originating from China is called the Knot of Eternity.

The five-pointed star is also called a pentagram. It attracts elementals and angels if the fifth point is upward. If it is down, it attracts distorted energy. It is a symbol of harmony, heath, and mystic powers; it will either trap or repel negative energy.

The six-pointed star is a pattern of two overlapping triangles, called a hexagram, Solomon's Seal, or the Star of David. It represents change and luck. Use it for protection through balancing opposites.

A seven-pointed star is also called a heptad, mystic star, or elvenstar or elf star. The number seven was also considered the most powerful and sacred of all numbers to the ancient Egyptians. It is excellent for contacting dragons and for indicating that you are ready to study with them. It activates healing energies. A protective symbol, this star can balance all the chakras. This star is also associated with the seven sisters of the Pleiades, a home planet to some of the dragon clans.

The eight-pointed star, or octagon, is a design beneficial for attracting strength and growth after traumatic events. It switches the life path into a new cycle. It also can correct and balance karma.

A nine-pointed star is the traditional symbol of a spiritual initiation. It is filled with great power because it is composed of three joined triangles. Use it to end one cycle and begin a new one. It protects all who use it.

The ten-pointed star symbolizes satisfactory completion. It is very useful in magick that affects your career or a future job.

The twelve-pointed star is a direct representation of the zodiac and astrology. Each point signifies a zodiacal house of an astrological chart. Activate the energy of this star by tracing its lines in a clockwise direction. By doing this, you can minimize the negative effects of a situation.

Stones by Color

The power of stones can be used by placing a stone near your candle while burning, or you can wear it in jewelry. The stone emanates certain vibrational powers that add to the energy you are needing. For more in-depth information on stones and herbs, check my previous two dragon books. Certain types of stones have their own individual powers also.

White: spiritual guidance, moon magick, visions, divination, dreams

Red: energy, courage, defense, physical love, sexuality, strength, power

Pink: true love, friendship, relaxation, calming, smooth difficulties, build self-love, peace, happiness

Yellow: power and energy of the mind, creativity of the mental type, sudden changes, communication skills, heighten visualization, travel

Orange: changing luck, power, protection by control of a situation, illumination, personal power, building self-worth, attract luck and success

Blue: healing, harmony, understanding, journeys or moves, peace, calm emotion, stop nightmares, restful sleep, purification of the inner being

Green: growth, fertility, money, marriage, good health, grounding, balancing

Brown: amplifies all earth magick and psychic abilities

Black: general defense, binding, repelling dark magick, cursing, reversing thought-forms and spells into positive power

Purple: break bad luck, protection, success in long range plans, spiritual growth

Indigo and turquoise: discover past lives or karmic problems, balancing karma, new and unique ideas

Additional Stones for Magick

You will find more complete lists of stones and how to use their power in magick in *Dancing with Dragons* and *Mystical Dragon Magick*. However, these stones are especially powerful and important.

Agate, Fire: returns negativity to sender; helps you to intuitively read symbols and open yourself to spiritual gifts

Amber: rebirth and renewal

Amethyst: courage; strengthens relationships

Dragon Stone: also call Bastite. Activate creation on all levels, as well as dragon energy in the earth; brings order out of chaos

Fossil stones: any stone with fossilized remains of a plant or animal in them offer protection, balancing with earth energies, instruction on past lives, and guidance through other worlds

Geode: represents the dragon cave during initiation magick

Holey or holed stone: stones with a naturally formed hole in them; a symbol of the hole through time and space

Jasper, Dragon's blood: provides better connection to the dragons.

Labradorite: said to hold enchanted mysteries of the northern lights

Lodestone or Magnetite: draws power to attract what you want

Moonstone, Black: a type of labradorite. Protects and opens your energy field to high vibrations. Use to attract a spiritual guide.

Moonstone, Blue or White: high-vibrational stone that creates a subtle geometric, merkaba-shaped energy pathway to the physical brain

Moonstone, Rainbow: helps you to see the unseen, intuitively read symbols, and open yourself to spiritual gifts

Mother-of-Pearl, Black: Psychic ability

Opal, Ethiopian: high-vibrational stone that burns off karma of the past and opens the way for rebirth. Ancient wisdom.

Opal, White: mental clarity

Petrified Wood: fossilized ancient trees. Use for defense, setting up barriers, exploring past lives.

Pyrite: money, prosperity, total success; intensifies good luck

Quartz crystal: amplifies magickal power. All dragons are attracted to quartz.

Serpentine, Green: inner peace, quiet joys of nature

Staurolite: looks like an X or equal-armed cross; symbol of protection. Use for balance on all levels, such as money, good luck, wealth, good health.

Tanzanite: stone of magick; contains volcanic force

Tektite/Meteorite: helps to connect to star power and the universe; protection, traveling from one plane of existence to another

Turquoise, Blue and Purple: protection

Stone Batteries

It is always wise to keep small stone "batteries" available for emergency use, rather like the external batteries used to recharge cell phones and electronic tablets. The kind of stone doesn't really matter, although quartz crystals are the very best. However, you must be knowledgeable about the crystals as some cannot be used as batteries. Small ordinary stones work well for batteries and can be carried in a little pouch if you need to travel.

Hold the stones in your hands, rub them gently, and visualize dragon power flowing through you into the stones. Say:

> *Dragons of the elements,*
> *sun and moon, and every star,*
> *Pour your power into these stones,*
> *be you near, or be you far.*
> *Fill each tight, from edge to edge,*
> *with your energy pure and bright.*
> *Flood these stones with dragon breath,*
> *the Multiverse's strongest light.*

Put the empowered stones into a special bag. Then breathe gently into the bag to lock them to your vibrations. This prevents any other magician from using them.

You can use the energy from only one stone by holding it while chanting, or you can call upon all the stones by holding your hands above them. When calling upon the stone "batteries" to release their stored power, say:

> *Stones awaken. Answer my plea.*
> *Pour out your power. Work well for me.*

Use the Charm of Making at the end of a spell to make it more powerful.

> *By glow of Sun, the power's begun.*
> *By moonbeam's light, the spell is right,*
> *To create desire by Earth and Fire.*
> *Water, Air, make magick fair.*
> *Powerful Charm of Making,*
> *creative Magickal undertaking.*
> *By storm, be formed!*

Candle Colors

Black: discord, protection from retribution, power, willpower, strength, revenge, reversing, uncrossing, binding negative forces, protection, releasing, repel dark magick and negative thought-forms

Blue: truth, inspiration, wisdom, occult power, protection, understanding, good health, happiness, peace, fidelity, harmony in the home, patience

Blue-green: for the emotional side of these aspects. Iridescent blue: the spiritual side of these aspects.

Dark blue: definitely the moodier sides of these aspects

Brown: attract money and financial success; concentration, balance, ESP, intuition, study

Gold or very clear light yellow: great fortune, intuition, understanding, divination, fast luck, financial benefits, attracting higher influences

Green: abundance, fertility, good fortune, generosity, money, wealth, success, renewal, marriage, balance

Indigo or turquoise: meditation, neutralize another's magick; stop gossip, lies, or undesirable competition; out of balance karma

Magenta: very high vibrational frequency that tends to work fast, so it is usually burned with other candles. It is best for quick changes, spiritual healing, exorcism.

Orange: encouragement, adaptability, stimulation, attraction, sudden changes, control, power, to draw good things, changing luck

Pink: true love, affection, romance, spiritual awakening, healing of the spirit, togetherness

Purple: success, idealism, higher psychic ability, wisdom, progress, protection, honors, spirit contact, break a bad luck cycle, drive away evil, divination

Very dark purple: a difficult color to handle as your desires may turn into negative obsessions

Red: physical power, willpower, strength, purely physical sex. If not used with the correct intent, this may turn the energy into obsessions.

Silver or very clear light gray: removes negative powers; victory, stability, meditation, developing psychic abilities

White: purity, spirituality and higher attainments of life, truth, sincerity, power of a higher nature, wholeness

Yellow: intellect, imagination, power of the mind, creativity, confidence, gentle persuasion, action, attraction, concentration, inspiration, sudden changes

Special Quartz Crystals

Dragons seem to be very partial to quartz crystals, although they love all stones. Quartz has a very long magickal history on earth; I understand from the dragons that quartz crystals are prized on all the planets of the Multiverse.

The following list of descriptions will help you identify various types of quartz crystals. You will also find a magnifying glass and a blue pen light useful. I don't understand why blue shows the inclusions in quartz better; I just know from personal experience it does. The most interesting are not the ones that are absolutely clear, but the crystals that have inclusions and fractures inside them.

Abundance: one large pointed crystal with at least seven other small points around the base in a vertical position

Atlantean or Record Keepers: Record Keepers with equilateral triangles are said to have Atlantean records. Atlantis has been the marker for a very long time, especially for Arkansas crystals.

Channeling: sometimes called the "sage" of the crystal clan, this is a spiritual growth crystal with seven sides

Clusters: a formation consisting of a number of crystal points, all growing from a common base. Set your stones and crystals on this to recharge them.

Devic: usually has many internal fractures and inclusions. Sometimes the crystals have no points. The crystal contains a great number of internal fractures and inclusions that often reveal the forms of elves, faeries, other nature spirits, or animals.

Diamond window: a four-sided vertical diamond shape appears on or as one of the main faces. Usually quite clear.

Double-Terminated: a crystal with a termination on both ends

Dow: three seven-edged channel faces of the same size on the pointed tip, with alternating three same-sized triangles

Elestial: also called skeletal crystal. The features on this crystal are flat to nearly flat points, with irregular cut-in triangular spaced. It usually looked burned. It may contain drops of encapsulated water and have strange cryptic markings.

Enhydro: also called hydrolite, it contains drops of water

Etched: a crystal with natural geometric and/or hieroglyphic-looking marks

Fairy frost: inclusions of water, gases, air, and internal fractures; they have beautiful interior veils

Guide: sometimes called a dolphin. It has a much smaller, perfectly formed crystal attached naturally to one of the sides.

Herkimer diamond: found around Herkimer, New York, they are small, stubby, double-terminated crystals that usually very clear. Use them for dreams, visions, time travel, dimensional shifting, and to open dimensional doorways.

Isis face: the main face at the tip has five edges, like a triangle on top of a rectangle

Lemurian seed: Record Keepers with elongated or irregular triangles; they also must have horizontal stripelike grooves or striations on the sides. They often have natures etching that look like hieroglyphics. You can recover the information they contain by rubbing the grooves with your fingers while meditating.

Library: a crystal with a strange irregular formation of flat, stubby crystals on its side. These attachments are merely slight rises and don't have the usual crystalline shape.

Manifestation: also called Creators, because they contain another perfectly formed crystal completely inside it

Phantom, black: has a small black outline of a crystal point inside it

Phantom, white: has a small white outline of a crystal point inside. You can use it to access the Akashic Records and past-life memories; also helps connect with spirit guides.

Record Keeper: has a geometric symbol (usually a triangle) naturally etching into the sides or interior. Can be used to access ancient information as far back as Atlantis and Lemuria.

Rutilated: clear crystal containing thin strands of gold, titanium, asbestos, black tourmaline, or fossilized carbon

Spirit guardian: two double-terminated crystals naturally attached at the side, of equal or nearly equal length. Very personal crystals for connecting you with spirit teachers, guides, and guardians. Can also help you find ancient, forgotten knowledge.

Transmitter: has a prominent triangular face. On each side of this face are two seven-sides faces with a smaller seven-edged channel face opposite.

Veil: also called a wall crystal. It has an inner fracture or inclusion that completely divides the interior. This veil may appear solid or gauzy. Sometimes these crystals also have rainbows.

BOOKS OF INTEREST

Aima. *Perfume Oils, Candles, Seals, and Incense*. Los Angeles: Foibles Publications, 1981.

Ash, Heather. *The Four Elements of Change*. San Francisco: Council Oak Books, 2004.

Bailey, Alice. *Esoteric Astrology*. Three volumes. New York: Lucis, 1976.

Blavatsky, H. P. *Isis Unveiled*. [n.p.]: New York, 1887. Reprint, Secaucus, NJ: Citadel Press, 1980.

———. *The Secret Doctrine*. [n.p.]: New York, 1888. Reprint, Secaucus, NJ: Citadel Press, 1980.

Branston, Brian. *Gods and Heroes from Viking Mythology*. New York: Schocken Books, 1982.

Budge, E. A. Wallis. *Amulets and Superstitions*. London, 1930. Reprint, New York: Dover Publications, 1978.

Byfield, Barbara Ninde. *The Glass Harmonia*. London: Collier-Macmillan Ltd., 1967.

Campbell, Joseph. *Masks of God* vols 2 & 3. New York: Viking Press, 1963, 1964. Reprint, Penguin Books, 1976.

———. *The Power of Myth*. New York: Doubleday, 1988.

Cavendish, Richard, editor. *Mythology: An Illustrated Encyclopedia*. New York: Rizzoli, 1980.

Clow, Barbara Hand. *Chiron: Rainbow Bridge Between the Inner and Outer Planets*. St. Paul, MN: Llewellyn, 1999.

Corrigan, Ian. *The Book of the Dragon: A New Grimoire*. [n.l.]: J. L. Wyndham, 1983.

Cunningham, Scott. *The Complete Book of Incense, Oils and Brews*. St. Paul, MN: Llewellyn Publications, 1985.

Conway, D. J. *Crystal Enchantments*. Freedom, CA: The Crossing Press, 1999.

———. *Dancing with Dragons*. St. Paul, MN: Lewellyn, 2001.

———. *Elemental Magick*. Franklin Lakes, NJ: New Page Books, 2006.

———. *Mystical Dragon Magick*. Woodbury, MN: Llewellyn, 2008.

Daniels, Estelle. *Astrological Magick*. York Beach, ME: Samuel Weiser, 1995.

De A'Morelli, Richard, and Sharana Reavis. *The Book of Magickal & Occult Rites & Ceremonies*. West Nyack, NY: Parker Publishing, 1980.

Fontana, David. *The Secret Language of Symbols*. London: Duncan Baird, 1993.

Gayley, Charles Mills. *The Classic Myth in English Literature &In Art*. New York: Ginn and Company, 1939.

Gonzalez-Wippler, Migene. *The Complete Book of Amulets and Talismans*. St. Paul, MN: Llewellyn Publications, 1991.

Grimal, Pierre, editor. *Larouse Encyclopedia of Mythology*. London, 1959. Reprint, New York, Hamlyn, 1978.

Gwain, Shati. *Creative Visualization*. New York: Bantam Books, 1982.

Hall, Judy. *The Crystal Bible*. 3 volumes. Cincinnati, OH: Walking Stick Press, 2004.

———. *Crystals to Empower You*. Cincinnati, OH: Walking Stick Press, 2013.

Hall, Manly P. *The Secret Teachings of All Ages*. San Francisco, 1928. Reprint, Los Angeles, CA: Philosophical Research Society, 1977.

Hart, Francene. *Sacred Geometry Cards*. Rochester, VT: Bear and Company, 2008.

———. *Sacred Geometry Oracle Deck*. Rochester, VT: Bear and Company, 2001.

Hogarth, Peter. *Dragons*. New York: Viking Press, 1979.

Hoult, Janet. *Dragons: Their History & Symbolism*. Glastonbury, UK: Gothic Image, 1990.

Huxley, Francis. *The Dragon: Nature of Spirit, Spirit of Nature.* UK: Thames & Hudson, 1979.

Janse, Eva Rudy. *Singing Bowls.* Havelte, Netherlands: Binkey Kok, 1992.

Johnson, Cait. *Earth, Water, Fire & Air.* Woodstock, VT: Skylight Paths, 2003.

Kalweit, Holger. *Dreamtime and Inner Space.* Boston: Shambhala, 1988.

Lady Rhea, and Eve Le Fey. *The Enchanted Candle.* New York: Citadel Press, 2004.

Lambert, Mary. *Crystal Energy.* New York: Sterling, 2005.

Lum, Peter. *Fabulous Beasts.* New York: Pantheon Books, 1951.

MacKenzie, Donald G. *German Myths & Legends.* New York: Avenel, 1985.

McArthur, Margie. *Wisdom of Elements.* Freedom, CA: The Crossing Press, 1995.

Mickaharic, Draja. *Magickal Practice.* Tinicum, PA: xlibris, 2004.

Miller, Jason. *Protection and Reversal Magick.* Pompton Plains, NJ: The Career Press/New Page, 2006.

Murphy-Hiscock, Ann. *Power of Spellcraft for Life.* Avon, MA: Provenance Press, 2005.

Musashi, Miyamoto. *A Book of Five Rings: The Classic Guide to Strategy.* Woodstock, NY: Overlook Press, 1974.

Page, James Lynn. *Applied Visualization.* St. Paul, MN: Llewellyn Publications, 1991.

Pennick, Nigel. *Magickal Alphabets.* York Beach, ME. Samuel Weiser, 1992.

Perkins, John. *Shape Shifting.* Rochester, VT: Destiny Press, 1997.

Richardson, Wally, and Lenora Huett. *Spiritual Value of Gem Stones.* Marina del Rey, CA: De Vorss & Co, 1983.

Serraillier, Ian. *Beowulf the Warrier.* New York: Scholar Book Services, 1970.

Silbey, Uma. *The Complete Crystal Guidebook.* New York: Bantam, 1996.

Stearn, Jess. *The Power of Alpha-Thinking.* New York: New American Library, 1976.

Sun Tzu. *The Art of Strategy.* Translated by R. L. Wing. New York: Broadway Books, 2000.

Trayer, Patricia. *Crystal Personalities: A Quick Reference to Special Forms of Crystal.* Peoria, AZ: Stone People Publishing, 1995.

Tresidder, Jack. *Dictionary of Symbols.* San Francisco: Chronicle Books, 1998.

White, T. H. *The Book of Beasts.* New York: G. P. Putnam's Sons, 1954. Reprint, New York, Dover Publications, 1984.

Wolfe, Amber. *In the Shadow of the Shaman.* St. Paul, MN: Llewellyn Publications, 1990.

Zerner, Amy, and Monte Farber. *The Alchemist: The Formula for Turning Your Life into Gold.* New York: St. Martin's, 1991.

GET MORE AT **LLEWELLYN.COM**

Visit us online to browse hundreds of our books and decks, plus sign up to receive our e-newsletters and exclusive online offers.

- **Free tarot readings • Spell-a-Day • Moon phases**
- **Recipes, spells, and tips • Blogs • Encyclopedia**
- **Author interviews, articles, and upcoming events**

GET SOCIAL WITH **LLEWELLYN**

Find us on  @LlewellynBooks

www.Facebook.com/LlewellynBooks

GET BOOKS AT **LLEWELLYN**

LLEWELLYN ORDERING INFORMATION

Order online: Visit our website at www.llewellyn.com to select your books and place an order on our secure server.

Order by phone:
- Call toll free within the US at 1-877-NEW-WRLD (1-877-639-9753)
- We accept VISA, MasterCard, American Express, and Discover.

Order by mail:
Send the full price of your order (MN residents add 6.875% sales tax) in US funds plus postage and handling to: Llewellyn Worldwide, 2143 Wooddale Drive, Woodbury, MN 55125-2989

POSTAGE AND HANDLING

STANDARD (US):(Please allow 12 business days)
$30.00 and under, add $6.00.
$30.01 and over, FREE SHIPPING.

CANADA:
We cannot ship to Canada. Please shop your local bookstore or Amazon Canada.

INTERNATIONAL:
Customers pay the actual shipping cost to the final destination, which includes tracking information.

Visit us online for more shipping options. Prices subject to change.

FREE CATALOG!

To order, call
1-877-
NEW-WRLD
ext. 8236
or visit our
website